THE OMEGA GENERATION

A Handbook for Last Days' Believers

The Omega Generation:
A Handbook for Last Days' Believers

By Denise Haas, AKA Big D 2023
Email dhaasbigd@gmail.com for more information

All Scripture passages are quoted from the NASB unless otherwise noted.

ISBN: 979-8-218-96688-1

THEOMEGAGENERATION.COM
JUSTHOLDONBOOK.COM

This book is dedicated to the
Body of Christ in these last days.
Remain calm, and trust God.
We win and the prize is Jesus.

Contents

Preface

This book is divided into two main parts.

Part One is written to believers in Jesus who are alive **before** the seven seals are opened, and the seven-year Tribulation begins. Some in the Church are asleep and need to be awakened to what's happening so that we can all be prepared for the days to come (in Part Two). Currently, we are living as "last days' believers" and we are in a unique place. We are the last generation on planet earth. And while there may be some harrowing challenges ahead for us, there will also be a special grace that comes with these challenges. And like any good soldier, we'll need to be familiar with the specific equipment and (spiritual) weapons needed for the mission before us. It could very well be that today's tribulations are a training ground for the tomorrow's (Capital T) Tribulation.

Part Two is written to believers who are alive **after** the first seal is broken by Jesus and the seven-year tribulation begins. These are those who will go THROUGH a good portion of The Tribulation. Whether you believe in a pre-tribulation, mid-tribulation, or post-tribulation, what really matters is if we are prepared and equipped to navigate any scenario that we may find ourselves in in the end. I do not believe, under any circumstance that we will incur the "wrath of God" which entails the seven bowl judgments in Revelation 16:1-21. That being said, the seven seals and the seven trumpets are no walk in the park! After much study over the years, I can reasonably see Christians going through the seven seals, and the seven trumpets before the Lord *"catches us up," and "gathers" us together (*1 Thessalonians 4:17, 2 Thessalonians 2:1).

While the events of the seven-year Tribulation will be more severe than the world has ever seen before (which will include world-wide persecution and martyrdom for believers), they are not, in my opinion, the definition of the "Great" Tribulation. That will occur when God's judgment (wrath) and the devil's wrath are poured out simultaneously upon an unrepentant humanity (Revelation 16, 17, 18).

The point of this book is not to spark arguments over "when" these things will take place, but rather to help the Body of Christ to be encouraged and equipped for every good work in the midst of whatever times we may find ourselves.

May what is written here help us to love our Lord Jesus Christ always, whether we are in the small "t" tribulations of life or the capital "T" Tribulation of the end. God wrote many instructions for the "last days' believers." Clearly, these "final instructions" were NOT written for the people who wrote them thousands of years ago. I believe they were written for us, so this book will lean heavily on the Scriptures that speak specifically of the "last days," what we can expect, and how we should act when these things come to pass.

Are you ready? Let's go!

Introduction

Handbook: A concise manual or reference book providing specific information or instruction about a subject or place.

Omega means **"last"** in the Greek Language.

The Omega Generation is a handbook intended to help last days' believers to navigate these last days mainly through reminders from the Scriptures.

It's not a novel or a book for **entertaining**, but rather, it's a training manual for **equipping** the saints for the work of ministering in and to this last generation.

It's intended to be a guide to the "How-To's, Don't Do's, and the What-to-Do's when stuff begins to happen that we couldn't even fathom before.

The Omega Generation will be 'heavy' on the Scriptures, so, even if you find yourself not as excited about these verses as you ought to be, I can tell you that when the time comes, these very Scriptures will come alive to us, and we will all be feeding on them, and depending upon them as if our very lives depended upon every word, because they will.

Per my instructions from the Lord, I will try very hard to be concise, and give only the commentary that the Lord leads me to add.

I pray that this handbook is all that God intended it to be to equip believers to thrive in these final days. As the last generation of humankind as we know it, let's finish well, and help others to do the same.

Let's remain calm, and trust God. **We are the Omega Generation, and we are almost home.**

Shalom,

Big D

Part One: the Divine Timeline

(Before the first seal is broken)

Chapter 1: *Are we in the "last days?"*

*"God, after He spoke long ago to the fathers in the prophets in many portions and in many ways, **in these last days** has spoken to us in His Son, whom He appointed heir of all things, through whom also He made the world."* Hebrews 1:1-2

But first, Jesus.

*"Now as they were traveling along, He (Jesus) entered a village; and a woman named Martha welcomed Him into her home. **And she had a sister called Mary, who was also seated at the Lord's feet, and was listening to His word.** But Martha was distracted with all her preparations; and she came up to Him and said, 'Lord, do You not care that my sister has left me to do the serving by myself? Then tell her to help me.' But the Lord answered and said to her, 'Martha, Martha, you are worried and distracted by many things; but only one thing is necessary; for Mary has chosen the good part, which shall not be taken away from her.'"* Luke 10:38-42

We begin this handbook with the **one thing** that's necessary, spending time at Jesus' feet—listening to His word. We will not be ready for this day, or this year, or what's coming if we don't listen to the voice of our Good Shepherd every minute of every hour of every day. It's in His presence that everything makes sense. It's the "good part" of the day where we give Him thanks and praise, and where we receive the strength and wisdom necessary for our lives. If we spend that quality time at Jesus' feet in the morning, the rest of the day is just the overflow of His presence as we walk in the good works that He's prepared for us to walk in (Ephesians 2:10). Thankfully, Jesus has uncomplicated our walk with God, and has simplified it for us by boiling it all down to one thing—*Seek first the* **King***dom of God and His righteousness (Jesus is our righteousness), and all the other things will be added to us* (Matthew 6:33). When we start to become confused, worried or distracted by the circumstances of our lives, there's still always only "one thing that's necessary," and that is, spending time at Jesus' feet. In these last days, God has spoken to us through His Son. Let's take time every day to Shema (hear) what He's saying to us.

*"...But this is what was spoken of through the prophet Joel: 'And it shall be in **the last days**,' God says, 'That I will pour forth of My Spirit on all mankind; and your sons and your daughters shall prophesy, and your young shall see visions, and your old shall dream dreams; Even on My bondslaves, both men and women, I will in those days pour forth of My Spirit and they shall prophesy.'"* Acts 2:16-18 and Joel 2:28-29

Are we in the last days? Let's talk football. The Two-Minute Warning

I like football. I used to watch it a lot with my grandma in my teenage years. Truth be told, if I could have played football, I would have. But alas, I am a girl, and much to my disappointment, they never made a female football league.

I almost always root for the underdog. Maybe that's because, in my life, I've felt like an underdog at times, and maybe that's just human nature to want to see the weak or the small rise up and win. To that point, since childhood, I have rooted for the Detroit Lions. I know, I know, they have never even made it to a Super Bowl, much less win one.

Now, besides rooting for the underdog, I love to see teams come from behind. The Green Bay Packers were such a team when I was growing up. They would be way behind at the half and losing all the way to the very last minute and then they would pull off a football miracle. Good times.

I think most teams do their best work in the last two minutes of the game. For those who don't know much about football, this is called the "two-minute" warning.

At this point, there is a pause or a break before the final two-minute countdown. This is where the rubber meets the road. It all comes down to these last minutes. They can't buy more time, and they try not to waste any time. If the score is close, it's in those final two minutes that everything can change, and quickly.

In a Super Bowl, careers are on the line. So, it behooves these players to be ready for the game. There's no more time to practice. No more time to study the other team's film. There's no time to strategize or to rest. If you don't know what you're doing by now, the pressure of these final two minutes can absolutely ruin your chances of winning. Those who are disciplined and practiced are the ones who will excel under such pressure. If they're not ready, it will show up in their play at the end of the game.

In our continuing study of the Book of Revelation, we are seeing some things that make me think that we are very close to the end of this "game" so to speak, and Jesus is coming back soon. In response to that statement, some might say, such as they have said for the last 2000 years, **"Where is this 'coming' He promised? Ever since our**

ancestors died, everything goes on as it has since the beginning of creation." 2 Peter 3:4 (NIV) (We'll talk about Mockers in a few minutes.) But just a few verses down in verse 8, Peter makes a curious statement, **"But do not let this one fact escape your notice, beloved, that with the Lord one day is like a thousand years and a thousand years like one day." 2 Peter 3:8 (NIV)**

In 2017, I brought this equation to a mathematician. Here's what she concluded. *"If a day is as a thousand years to the Lord and a thousand years is as one day, then how long are our lives if we live to be eighty years of age? The answer is:* **One hour and fifty-five minutes for eighty years, and one hour and forty-one minutes for seventy years of life."** Hmmm.

Two thousand years ago, Peter quoted the prophet Joel when he said, **"In the last days, God says, I will pour out my Spirit on all people. Your sons and daughters will prophesy, your young will see visions, your old will dream dreams."** Peter went on to say that this Scripture was being fulfilled right then and there. (Acts 2:14-21) So, that means the **"last *days"*** started almost 2000 years ago!

Then in 1 John 2:18 (which was written approximately 30 years after Acts, chapter 2), we're told that it was the **"last hour."** Add to that, all of the signs of the "times," which we would have to admit, since 2020, are different from any other time in history mostly because events are taking place on a global scale, and you have the makings for the end of all things as we know it.

If we follow the equation, mankind only has a few minutes left on the clock before the "game" is over. The fact is, this is far from a game. What we do with Jesus in these last few minutes will determine our eternity!

I could be right about the timing, but even if I'm not, Jesus is still coming back. Even He said it would be soon (According to the equation, Jesus has only been gone for two days).

My advice to all of us is to look at our lives. Are we right with God? Are we poised to "win?" Have we been "practicing" our walk with God? Or are we falling apart under the pressure of this life?

It's time to get serious about the end of all things because we are all in the eternal Super Bowl, and the prize is eternity with God.

So, whether Jesus comes back, or we die first, we're going to want to be ready.

Please don't put it off. There's no time to waste. We could be at the **Two-Minute Warning**, and Jesus wants us to win by knowing Him.

The Doomsday Clock

So, *are* we in the last days?
For reasons different from that of the Bible, these people seem to think so.

"Founded in 1945 by Albert Einstein and University of Chicago scientists who helped develop the first atomic weapons in the Manhattan Project, the Bulletin of the Atomic Scientists created the Doomsday Clock two years later, using the imagery of apocalypse (midnight) and the contemporary idiom of nuclear explosion (countdown to zero) to convey threats to humanity and the planet. The Doomsday Clock is set every year by the Bulletin's Science and Security Board in consultation with its Board of Sponsors, which includes 10 Nobel laureates. The Clock has become a universally recognized indicator of the world's vulnerability to global catastrophe caused by manmade technologies." https://thebulletin.org/doomsday-clock/

The clock's original setting in 1947 was seven minutes to midnight. It has since been set backward eight times and forward 16 times for a total of 24, the farthest from midnight being 17 minutes in 1991, and the nearest being 100 seconds in 2020.

The clock was moved to two and a half minutes in 2017, then forward to two minutes to midnight in January 2018, and left unchanged in 2019. In January 2020, it was moved forward to 100 seconds before midnight. The clock's setting was left unchanged in both 2021 and 2022. Since 2010, the clock has been moved forward over four minutes, and has changed by five minutes and twenty seconds since 1947.

At the time of this writing, October 2023, the doomsday clock is at **90 seconds to midnight.**

A time of unprecedented Danger!
2023 Doomsday Clock Statement

Science and Security Board
Bulletin of the Atomic Scientists

(https://thebulletin.org/doomsday-clock/current-time/)

The Survey Says!

Surveys are the bomb!

Thanks to the others who joined with me from the "Preach! Jesus" study in sharing this survey. I had some very good discussions as I administered it to several people; especially with those who did not claim to be born-again. I found that this survey could be used as a tool to whet the person's appetite for spiritual things, and to spark an urgency regarding one's eternal destination.

Here are the simple, and uncomplicated findings of my unscientific survey:

*Surprisingly, not everyone thinks we are in the last days, but most agree that some unprecedented things happened (such as lock-downs) in 2020 that had never occurred before, and that this shift was worldwide. Also, the generation of today is called, **Gen Z.** (Interesting...the last letter of our English alphabet...perhaps it's the last generation?) Maybe we are the Omega generation, after all.

*On a scale from 1 to 10 with 10 being a boatload of peace, whatever number they put down (none below 6) they attributed that level of peace to God.

*Also surprising to me was the amount of people who said that it wouldn't bother them if we were in the last days, but these were mainly the same folks who, in answer to the question, "If Jesus were to come back today, would you be prepared or unprepared?" responded that they would be unprepared.

*Those being surveyed were asked to describe their relationship with God:

a. Very close b. Somewhat close c. Distant d. Non existent

It was alarming to me that some who said "somewhat close" also stated that they would be "unprepared" if He came back today.

*And finally, in answer to the question, "What qualifies a person to go to heaven?"

a. Good works b. I'm not as bad as murderers, etc.
c. Trusting only in the sacrifice Jesus made on the cross,

Almost everyone picked **C** even though they stated that they would be unprepared if He came back today. (Only **C** is correct. *If you don't know Him, please call out to Jesus, trusting only in His sacrifice on the cross, and ask Him to save you).*

*Only a couple of people said that it was "good works" that qualify us to go to heaven.

I've printed the survey in this book so that you can give it to others as a witnessing tool. Please don't just hand it to someone, and walk away. If possible, please print this survey and treat it as an interview. Those to whom I gave the survey were glad to talk about their answers. Who knows if someone you're interviewing won't realize that they are "unprepared" for Jesus' return and that they are not trusting in Jesus in order to qualify for heaven, and right on the spot, accept Jesus as their Lord? It could happen. I pray that it does.

You can find the survey sheet at the back of this book, on page 121

*"Know this first of all, that **in the last days mockers will come** with their mocking, following after their own lusts, and saying, 'Where is the promise of His coming? For ever since the fathers fell asleep, all continues just as it was from the beginning of creation.'"* 2 Peter 3:3-4

Still, some are not convinced that we are currently in the last days. Perhaps they're afraid because they aren't right with God, I don't know, but one thing is sure, Christ followers should not be mocking God's timing. Instead, we ought to be "**...eagerly awaiting a Savior from there [Heaven], the Lord Jesus Christ....**" Philippians 3:20 (NIV)

Are You a Mocker?

People have been saying that the Lord is coming back "soon" since Jesus came the first time, 2000 years ago, I get it. In the Old Testament, they were looking for the Messiah to come. Then, when He did, many of the people did not recognize or receive Him. This reaction was prophesied, of course, in Isaiah 53:3, *"He was despised and rejected by people..."* And John 1:11 *"He came to His own, and His own did not receive Him."*

It is my opinion that every generation of Christians is supposed to think that we are the **last** generation. We are to look for His coming with great anticipation, and to the reality of His imminent return as our blessed hope. This faith perspective will cause us to live rightly AND to preach the good news of forgiveness with great urgency and passion.

The Apostle Peter wrote:

"But the day of the Lord will come like a thief. The heavens will disappear with a roar; the elements will be destroyed by fire, and the earth and everything done in it will be laid bare. Since everything will be destroyed in this way, what kind of people ought you to be? You ought to live holy and godly lives as you look forward to the day of God and speed its coming. That day will bring about the destruction of the heavens by fire, and the elements will melt in the heat. But in keeping with His promise we are looking forward to a new heaven and a new earth, where righteousness dwells." 2 Peter 3:10-13 (NIV)

Peter wasn't the only one who encouraged us to live like ours is the last generation. In answer to the question, *"When will the end come?"* Jesus answered, *"Of that day or hour no one knows, not even the angels in heaven, nor the Son, but the Father alone. Take heed, keep on the alert; for you do not know when the appointed time will come."* Matthew 24:36

The Time is Near *Near: at hand, within reach, soon*

*Luke 12:40 - *"You too, be ready; for the Son of Man is coming at an hour that you do not expect."*

*James 5:8 - *"You too be patient; strengthen your hearts, for the coming of the Lord is near."*

*Revelation 1:3 - *"Blessed is the one who reads, and those who hear the words of the prophecy and keep the things which are written in it; for the time is near."*

*Romans 13:11-12 — *"And do this, understanding the present time: The hour has already come for you to wake up from your slumber, because our salvation is nearer now than when we first believed. The night is nearly over; the day is almost here. So let us put aside the deeds of darkness and put on the armor of light."* (NIV)

*1 John 2:18 - *"Dear children, this is the last hour; and as you have heard that the antichrist is coming, even now many antichrists have come. This is how we know it is the last hour."* (NIV)

Note: We may not know the "day or the hour" of Jesus' return, but just as we can guess that a pregnant woman will give birth (on average) 12-24 hours after she goes into labor, Jesus gave us some signs that will show us when those "birth pangs" of His return will begin. (See Mark 13:7-8)

Now, back to our mockers...the "mockers" who are following after their own lusts, are also mistaken when they say, *"... For ever since the fathers fell asleep, all things continue just as they were from the beginning of creation."* This statement by the "mockers" is not true. I think some things *are* different from 2000 years ago, or 20 years ago, and even three years ago. I believe that 2020 marked a worldwide shift that catapulted us into the very last minutes of the last days. Since 2020, we have seen things, especially in the U.S., that are unprecedented.

Most who study the "end times" believe that America is not mentioned in the prophecy of the end. I agree with that assessment. In the very end, all eyes will be focused on Israel. Russia and China will rise to become major players, and we (the USA) will no longer be a super-power on the world's stage.

But even if this is not the end, God wants His people to live like it is. In the sense that the expectation of the soon coming of Jesus causes us to live soberly, faithfully, in holiness, love, and hopeful anticipation through prayer.

We need the kind of mindset that moves us to keep our focus on being prepared and helping others to take the "coming of the Lord" seriously, effectively silencing the mockers (and repenting if we've been a mocker). It's imperative that we tell everyone of this impending doom AND of the Gospel—whether this is the end of THE world, or it's the end of THEIR world, we will tell the Good News that Jesus made it possible for our sins to be forgiven and that we can be right with God through faith in the death and resurrection of Jesus. This is the most timely message ever told, and the greatest news ever! *Don't be a mocker. Be an expectant believer.*

Remain Calm & Trust God

*"For our citizenship is **in heaven**, from which we also eagerly wait for a Savior, the Lord Jesus Christ..."*
Philippians 3:20

It started for me in 2020. That was the year when everything shifted, and we saw unprecedented change happening on a global scale. That was the year that the whole world stopped. In America, we lost rights we forgot we even had. All of this led to a lot of US (myself included) being frustrated, confused and angry at the "world systems" that were at work in our country as well as all across the planet.

One day, I read this verse in Daniel, *"Many will be **purged, purified and refined**, but the wicked will act wickedly; and none of the wicked will understand, but those who have insight will understand."* Daniel 12:10 I realized that the "rights" I thought I had as a United States citizen were at best, secondary, to the rights I had as a citizen of heaven.

The Lord tells us in Philippians 3:20 (printed above) that the child of God doesn't have **dual citizenship** with the world, and therefore our rights and all of our hope (expectation for a good future) are not wrapped up in the things of this earth (Colossians 3). That's not to say that we can't use the "citizenship card" if we have to (Remember Paul used his Roman citizenship once when they were beating him without a trial - Acts 22:25). Still, when I remembered where my citizenship really lies, it helped me immensely. The verse in Daniel says, *"Many will be purged, purified and refined..."* I think the "Many" are the Last Days' Believers. Us. God disciplines those whom He loves. He doesn't purge, purify and refine the wicked. It goes on to say that the wicked won't understand what's going on, but those who have insight (believers in God) will. I finally realized that the pain I was feeling through losing my "rights" was a very needed purging, purifying, and refining that will strip me of any and all pride and equip me with humility; helping me to focus on the "things above" so that I will be able to be at peace in these terrible times. This world is not my home, but I found out in 2020 that I had deeper roots in it than I had ever imagined. I had been conformed to the world in some very real ways, and this was not squaring with my life in Christ, ergo, the increasing anger that I was experiencing. The year 2020 was only a taste of things to come.

As I tried to make sense of what was happening all around us, I became angry. Who did these people think they were? Now, I may sound like a rebel, but I assure you I am not. I just want there to be some logic to the rules. And the more that logic was consistently absent, I became increasingly suspicious and even angrier. When the "authorities" don't line up with what God has said, I guess you can call me a rebel because I'm never going to comply with any lie. Still, I was not at peace. And that's where Psalm 37 came to my rescue.

Do Not Fret!

Fret: in the Hebrew, this word means to "blaze up" as in fire-hot, wrath, anger.

It would be good to read the whole Psalm, but there is one truth that is repeated a few times in this Psalm that has helped me and is helping me still. Psalm 37:1 *"**Do not fret** because of evildoers..."* and Psalm 37:8 *"Cease from anger, and forsake wrath; **do not fret, it only leads to doing evil.**"*

In these last times, the people of God will need to maintain our peace and trust in Jesus. It's actually part of our good witness to unbelievers, and our encouragement to fellow believers. But how can we "not fret" in a world of evildoers?

Psalm 37 is chock full of ways **not** to fret:

Trust in the Lord

Commit your way to the Lord

Rest in the Lord

Delight yourself in the Lord

Wait for the Lord

The Lord helps, delivers, rescues, and blesses the one who keeps their eyes on Him.

God is Holding Your Hand

And finally, the verses in this Psalm that I love so much are found in Psalm 37:23-24 *"The steps of a person are established by the Lord; and He delights in his way. When he falls, he shall not be hurled headlong; because the Lord is the One who holds his hand."*

As we enter these times of The Tribulation, let's not fret. Instead, let's pray and remember that *it's all in the plan, we need to stay together, stay the course, stand firm, submit to God — resist the devil, hold fast to the Word of Life, preach Jesus, seek first God's Kingdom, cast all our cares upon Jesus, pray about everything, if it's a care—it's a prayer, give thanks in and for everything, do not fear, be courageous, hold on, and don't let go. But even if we do let go, know that the Lord, Himself, is holding our hand through it all. We have God's word on it.*

And when things begin to spin wildly out of our control, above all,

Remain Calm & Trust God

Chapter 2: Church! Wake Up & Be Ready!

"'And it shall be in the last days,' God says, 'That I will pour forth of My Spirit on all mankind; and your sons and your daughters shall prophesy, and your young shall see visions, and your old shall dream dreams; Even on My bondslaves, both men and women, I will in those days pour forth of My Spirit and they shall prophesy.'" Acts 2:16-18 & Joel 2:28-29

According to the Scripture above, and now that we know we are in the last days, what did God say would happen?

God would pour out His Spirit.

Upon whom? Your sons and your daughters (and the male and female bondservants).

What would they do? Prophesy.

Who else would God pour out His Spirit upon? Your young and old.

What would they do? The young would see visions, and the old would dream dreams...

And this is where my dream comes in.

I am convinced that indeed, these are the "last days," and now, I'm going to share with you just one of the things that

God said would happen in these days as He pours out His Spirit upon all flesh, *"...your young will see visions, and your old will dream dreams..."* Acts 2:17

In 2020, I had two dreams in one night. The following is an account of those dreams as well as what I believe to be the interpretation of them.

I have named this experience, **"Wake Up & Heed the Message!"**

"Wake up, wake up, wake up!"

That's what I was yelling when
I woke up on June 13, 2020.
I was having a very disturbing dream.

In my dream, I walked down the stairs to my front door. It was not the kind of door that I actually have, though, because this door had a sliding bolt lock, and mine does not. Immediately I saw that the bolt lock was indeed in the locked position, but also in that split second, the door opened and this 8 to 9 foot tall faceless, black blob came bursting in. And it was after me. At the same time, I was hearing the fisted knuckles of a distraught human rapidly knocking as if they were trying to get in. I never saw where the knocking was coming from because the large, black, silent monster had covered me as it backed me into the bedroom where my husband still slept. I tried to scream, but very little was being produced in my throat. This attack was completely silent except for the desperate knocking and my weak screams. I woke up to my own voice saying,

"Wake up, wake up, wake up!"

At that point, the dream ended and I was a little shaken up but not terrified. Actually, considering how terrifying the dream was, I was kind of surprised that I wasn't more upset. I think it was around 4:30 in the morning after the dream that I got up, went to the bathroom, and proceeded to go downstairs. I guess I was going to check the lock on my door. As I descended I could see the soft glow of my tree light that had been left on from the night before. I opened some of the blinds and looked out into the darkness. Everything was calm and I could hear a few 'early birds' waking up singing their songs. I went to the door, looked at the lock, checked it with my hand, and found that it was indeed locked. But in my dream, locked or not it didn't matter. This got me to thinking, and I prayed, **"Lord, if I have opened up the door to any evil or fear in my life, I'm shutting it right here and now. I officially shut and lock any and all doors that I thought were locked but weren't, and with the authority vested in me by my Lord Jesus Christ, I close these doors, and lock them in Jesus' name."** After surveying the room and outside one more time, I went back to bed.

I must have lain there for a good 30 minutes, just trying to sort out what I had just experienced. I concluded that the giant, black kind of blobby thing with no face was probably the actual "spirit of fear" (Fear doesn't have a face until we give it one). It was trying to force its way into my life through an area I thought was locked to the enemy. My prayer of confession and then authoritative declaration took care of that. At first, I thought the incessant knocking could be another person who was running from that same spirit because they thought I could help them fight the black monster. But after more consideration, I think it was Jesus trying desperately to remind me that only He could help me. And that the only way to shut the door to the enemy was to open the door to Him through a prayer for help. I believe it *was* Him and that's why I woke up and prayed. Throughout the whole ordeal, I never felt any pain or physical discomfort. It only affected me emotionally and spiritually.

Then I slowly drifted off to sleep. Again.

In my second dream of the night, I found myself held captive by a group of people with guns. They were killing people at random, and I was going from place to place in the house trying to hide from them. They had on uniforms of some kind and they were very angry. They had taken about fifty or more people hostage and kept them in one room in the house. For some reason, I was trying to make something happen to help all of us escape. After narrowly escaping detection in the bathroom, I made my way to another bedroom where I hid in a small, but deep closet. I heard someone come into the room. I held my breath as they opened one of the closet's double doors. Even though I was as still as could be, this person with a machine gun had found me. However, it only took a second to realize that this person was a friend. She had on a *"captor's"* uniform, but *she* was looking to escape. She told me that she had overheard a conversation I was having earlier with some of my fellow captives, about how we could escape if we would only have faith, and ask God for help. I had been telling them about how the Lord was able to blind the eyes of our captors and we could walk right out the door. "Well, it was possible," I said. "It had been done in the Bible in the Book of Acts." She said that she was willing to believe that truth, and asked if I would walk out of the door with her to get some help. "Sure," I said. So we proceeded to walk right by the people with guns, and past our captors as if we were invisible to them. As we made our way past our fellow captives, they all just stared at us with their mouths wide open. We exited the house, then the property, and then we knew that we were home free. The moment we turned the corner, we jumped up and down and hugged one another praising God because He had just saved our lives.

In my dream, we found ourselves outside of a duplex where I used to live in Florida. We were on our "Christian" neighbor's side of the duplex. They were alone and they listened to our story. However, they did not believe what we were saying. It was not too long after we arrived that their home started to fill up with people. They were having a graduation party for their son, and for some reason they were oblivious to the evil that was happening on the other side of their walls, right next door!

It was at this time that my husband came back to bed, having been awakened not long after my first dream. What

I learned from **the second dream** was that most people won't hear with ears of faith, and therefore, they will remain captives and eventually be killed by the enemy. Also, I should keep giving the message of freedom because I may not realize whom the Lord is trying to set free. It could be that He wants to save one of my captors! Unexpected deliverance. I shouldn't try to figure it out, and only preach to the people I think will listen. I should just keep giving the Good News of Jesus' salvation and freedom to everyone. That's my job as a follower of Jesus.

Recently, in our Revelation study, we were looking at Daniel 9:20-23, and specifically the last part of verse 23 which says, "*At the beginning of your supplications the command was issued, and I have come to tell you, for you are highly esteemed; so give heed to the message and gain understanding of the vision.*"

I was struck with that line that the angel Gabriel spoke to Daniel, "*...so give heed to the message....*" How was Daniel supposed to "heed" *that* message? Especially since it was not even a message for his time and he would never see it come to pass? Well, in this instance the only way Daniel could **heed** the message was to write it down, which he did, and which we are now studying.

I realized that the dreams did not only apply to me, but to the Body of Christ at large. Here's the message, and as for the heeding of it, each person must listen carefully to what the Spirit is saying to them and then act upon it.

Please listen carefully. Many of us are living our lives on this earth thinking that the doors to evil are shut and locked, but the truth is, we are being deceived. In the natural realm the doors **are** locked, but not so in the spiritual realm.

Jesus said this in John 14:30, "*I will not speak much more with you, for the ruler of the world is coming, and he has nothing in Me...*" We see that the devil has nothing "in" Jesus. He's got no part in Him, of Him, or on Him. We, however, as flawed human beings, sometimes have sin in our lives. Doors to evil are opened by our own sin. Sometimes, those doors that we thought were shut and locked are actually the things that give the devil the right to barrel into our lives and wreak havoc upon our hearts. Does the devil have something in you? Does he have something "on" you? If so, before we can heed the messages that God gives to us or even receive the messages that He wants to give to us, we must be clean and clear of any of the devil's hold on us. 1 John 1:9 says, "*If we confess our sins, He is faithful and just to forgive our sins and cleanse us from all unrighteousness.*" The enemy would lie to us and tell us that we need years of counseling or a month of fasting to be forgiven and set free from some of these strongholds, but I believe this scripture is saying that deliverance is as close as a prayer to God for forgiveness! Once we know we've sinned, let's confess it right away, and don't hold onto it. If we believe this one verse, we can be cleansed as often as we need to be, and we will be useful in this fight for souls in these last days.

The times are evil and they are going to get worse. After my first dream, I confessed any and every sin that I could think of, and asked the Lord to forgive me. I often pray these verses in Psalm 139:23-24 *"Search me, O God, and know my heart; Try me and know my anxious thoughts; And see if there be any wicked way in me, and lead me in the everlasting way."*

After my prayers of confession, I, personally, shut the door and locked it to the enemy through my declaration. We may have to do this on a daily basis to keep our vessels clean for our master's use in these final days.

Church, we are the first and last line of defense against the enemy of our souls, our nation, and our world. If we don't pray, this world doesn't have a prayer. Heed the message today. Get clean in your soul, spend time with God to hear what the Lord is saying, then do whatever it takes to heed the message that He's personally giving to you. Don't compare yourself with others, or try to model someone else's relationship with God. There's far too much of that. *You* can hear directly from God. **"Draw near to God and He will draw near to you...."** James 4:8

The one who presses into God is the one who is going to hear the most, be the closest and be used in the most amazing ways by God in this time. Jesus' will for us is not just that we bear fruit, but that we bear **much** fruit, and in that our heavenly Father will be glorified. (John 15:8)

And *always speak with faith and preach* the Gospel, because we never know who's listening. It could be an enemy whom God wants to save and transform to become one of His servants! No one is too far gone, and if they are, it's none of our business. We're in the business of our Father, and we're employed by Him to share the good news that Jesus can set people free from fear or anything else that seeks to destroy us. Furthermore, we don't do any of this in our own strength, but by God's Spirit we will overcome. And let's not forget that we must fight spiritual battles with spiritual weapons as we are dressed in God's spiritual armor:

"For though we walk in the flesh, we do not war according to the flesh, for the weapons of our warfare are not of the flesh, but divinely powerful for the destruction of fortresses. We are destroying speculations and every lofty thing raised up against the knowledge of God, and we are taking every thought captive to the obedience of Christ..." 2 Corinthians 10:3-5

"Finally, be strong in the Lord and in his mighty power. Put on the full armor of God, so that you can take your stand against the devil's schemes. For our struggle is not against flesh and blood, but against the rulers, against the authorities, against the powers of this dark world and against the spiritual forces of evil in the heavenly realms. Therefore put on the full armor of God, so that when the day of evil comes, you may be able to stand your ground, and after you have done everything, to stand. Stand firm then..." Ephesians 6:10-13a (NIV)

Recap: Message for the Church (Believers):

1. Wake up! (Remember 1 Thessalonians 5:4-9, and be sober and alert. The Lord is almost here!)

2. Lock your doors to the enemy, and keep them locked by remaining spiritually clean (Through confession and right living. Don't allow the enemy to have anything "in" you, "on" you, or "over" you. Stay alert in prayer always.)

3. Heed the message that God is giving to you. (Be obedient to God. Be a doer of His words. Don't compare your walk or gifts with anyone else in the Body of Christ.)

4. Keep preaching Jesus! (To everyone even if they don't look like they're listening or that they want to hear what we're saying. We may be talking to one person, but someone else is listening. How cool is that?)

"The night is almost gone, and the day is near. Therefore let us lay aside the deeds of darkness and put on the armor of light." Romans 13:12

*"But you, brothers and sisters, are not in darkness so that this day should surprise you like a thief. You are all children of the light and children of the day. We do not belong to the night or to the darkness. So then, let us not be like others, who are asleep, but let us be **awake and sober.** For those who sleep, sleep at night, and those who get*

drunk, get drunk at night. But since we belong to the day, let us be sober, putting on faith and love as a breastplate, and the hope of salvation as a helmet. For God did not appoint us to suffer wrath but to receive salvation through our Lord Jesus Christ." 1 Thessalonians 5:4-9 (NIV)

Bee Alert - Bee vigilant - Find the Entry Point - Seal it Up

Not only should we be awake, alert and ready for the Lord's return, but we should also be **on the alert** for the devil's attacks. As I have been writing this book, bees have been invading my house. At first, it was a major distraction as I tried to let them out. Three bees would come in (out of nowhere it seemed), I would let them out, then two more would come, and so on. Needless to say, I didn't get a lot of writing done that day. But that wasn't the main problem. The issue was that I had a mystery on my hands as I sought to find the "entry point" for those bees. (The 'bees' turned out to be hornets!) I guess if you want to distract me, just give me a mystery to solve. I spent most of the day trying to ascertain the entry point, and finally, I found it! But even after "plugging the hole," they were still coming. It turns out that the hornets had made a nest up by the roof in the facia. There was one, little crack, and they were getting into the attic. From there they were traveling through the house and finding the ONE entry point into my living space. And even though I thought I had plugged the hole, I did not do a thorough job of it. I finally got wise, and taped some plastic over the hole, but today, they are coming in with a vengeance, and from another place, too. Thankfully, my Father-In-Law was able to help me and he sprayed both the nest and the attic.

The enemy is just like those hornets. He will find the smallest crack in our walk with Jesus, and begin to invade our personal space. Even to the point of making a nest in our lives. The cracks that exist are created by the source of sin in our lives; sins such as: unforgiveness, bitterness, excessive anger, greed, immorality, pride, and addiction (of all kinds-to TV, alcohol, social media, our phones, pornography, witchcraft, etc.). Still, the biggest, most welcoming crack that the enemy of our souls will exploit is our lack of time spent with our Savior, Jesus.

Seal up the Hole with Time with the Holy One

Confession of sin, repentance, and "sinning no more" will do the job of sealing the gaping holes in our spiritual house, but our time with God is the main way that we can permanently destroy the nest of the enemy. Our time in God's presence is of the utmost importance if we want to be clean and useful vessels in God's Kingdom in these last times. If we're not spending quality time in God's presence every single day, we are at risk of temptation that will lead to sin. It only takes a short time for the evil one to use our compromise and lack of time with God to build another nest of sin in our lives. Remember what Jesus said to His disciples? *"Pray that you may not enter into temptation.*

The Spirit is willing, but the flesh is weak." That means, prayer and intimate time spent with God will keep us from being tempted in the first place. And when we are not wasting time being distracted and stumbling around in the dark through temptation, we can go on with the Father's business of going from strength to strength, from faith to (more) faith, and from glory to glory. *"The end of all things is near; therefore, be of sound judgment and sober spirit for the purpose of prayer."* 1 Peter 4:7

The Second Coming of Jesus & the Day of the Lord - One season of time?

As I've studied the end times for many years, I've come to believe that the **"Second Coming,"** and the **"Day of the Lord"** are one season of time. Just as Jesus' first coming consisted of His birth, life, death and resurrection which spanned about 33 years, I also think that Jesus' Second Coming will be a season of time that will last for seven years. It will include all of the events in the Book of Revelation (as well as several parallel passages in Daniel, Ezekiel, Zechariah, Matthew 24, 1 Thessalonians 4, and 2 Thessalonians 2). When Jesus opens the first Seal (Revelation 6), that will begin the **"Second Coming of Jesus"** which will include: **the Tribulation** (Seals & Trumpets, the anti-Christ's rise, martyrdom of believers, and more), **the Rapture** (the catching away of believers), **the seven bowl judgments** (the Great Tribulation), and finally, **the "Day of the Lord"** when Jesus comes to the earth riding on a white horse as described in Revelation 19, which is printed on page 96 of this book.

Every seal that's opened, and every trumpet that's blown will unveil another level of the terrifying power of Jesus. By the time the seven bowls of wrath are poured out upon whatever is left of humanity, there will not be any doubt as to Who Jesus is — the King of kings, and the Lord of lords.

Human beings are curious. God made us this way. That fact being established, ever since Jesus mentioned that there would be an end, His followers have sought to figure out the timeline. If only we had a **"Timeline Treasure Map...."** As you well know, The Bible is such a treasure map for many things including, but not limited to, the signs of the timing of His coming. We *can* certainly *understand* a lot more than we *can't understand* about the second coming of Jesus and the Day of the Lord. Here are just a few facts regarding what it will be like before, during, and after the Day of the Lord.

How Will The Day of the Lord Come?

"Terror, pain, and anguish will seize them; they will writhe **like a woman in labor***. They will look at one another, their faces flushed with fear. Behold, the* **Day of the LORD** *is coming—cruel, with fury and burning anger—to make the earth a desolation and to destroy the sinners within it."* Isaiah 13:8-9 (BSB)

*"Now concerning the times and the seasons, brothers and sisters, you have no need to have anything written to you. For you yourselves are fully aware that the **day of the Lord** will come **like a thief** in the night. While people are saying, "There is peace and security," then sudden **destruction** will come upon them **as labor pains come upon a pregnant woman,** and they will not escape."* 1 Thessalonians 5:1-3

*"But **the day of the Lord** will come **like a thief**, in which the heavens will pass away with a roar and the elements will be destroyed with intense heat, and the earth and its works will be burned up."* 2 Peter 3:10

How close is it? And will it be pleasant for "unbelievers?"
*"For the day is **near**, even **the day of the Lord** is **near**; It will be a day of clouds, **a time of doom for the nations**."* Ezekiel 30:3

Because this book is mainly focused on the preparedness of the child of God in these last days, I won't go into much more of the details of the signs and timing and such. Suffice it to say, to quote Ezekiel, the Prophet, **"The end is near!"**

Can we know exactly when it will come?

"THE CLOSER WE GET TO THE CITY, THE MORE SIGNS WE SEE."

"But about that day and hour no one knows, not even the angels of heaven, nor the Son, but the Father alone." Matthew 24:36

To Reiterate: Over the years, I've heard a good many people quote that '*No one knows the day or the hour*' verse in Matthew so as to say that we can never know what day or hour Jesus is coming back, so why worry about it at all? To which I say, **"It's not to worry about it, but to be prepared for it that matters."** Besides, I couldn't tell you the exact day nor the hour that I would give birth to my son, but I did know that it would be soon after I went into labor (it was 12 hours for me)! Let's be ready for what's coming, and urgently tell others this bad news so that they will see their need for the Good News of Jesus' beautiful, eternal salvation!

The Don'ts, the Do's, and the Be's for the Last Days' Believers

DON'T

DON'T *Don't get all wrapped up and obsessed in the details of the timing of the end.* **"He said to them: 'It is not for you to know the times or dates the Father has set by His own authority."** Acts 1:7 (NIV)

DON'T "*Don't have anything to do with godless myths and old wives' tales;* rather, **train yourself to be godly."** 1 Timothy 4:7 (NIV)

DON'T "Don't follow deceiving spirits and things taught by demons." 1 Timothy 4:1 (Summary)

DON'T "Don't be misled; for many will come in My name, saying, 'I am He,' and, 'The time is near.' **DON'T** go after them." Lk. 21:8 (NASB)

DON'T *"...Do not give up meeting together, as some are in the habit of doing, but encourage one another—and all the more as you see the Day approaching."* Hebrews 10:25 (NIV)

DON'T love money *"Those who want to get rich fall into temptation and a trap and into many foolish and harmful desires that plunge people into ruin and destruction. For the love of money is a root of all kinds of evil. Some people, eager for money, have wandered from the faith and pierced themselves with many griefs."* 1 Timothy 6:9 -10 (NIV)

DON'T mock the imminent and soon return of Jesus. 2 Peter 3:4, "In the last days, Mockers will come saying, **'Where is the promise of His coming? For all goes on exactly as it has since the beginning...'"**

DO Prophesy! *"...in the last days God will pour out His Spirit on all flesh.... and they will prophesy."* Acts 2:17 (NIV)

DO Avoid these kinds of people: *"...lovers of self, lovers of money, boastful, arrogant, revilers, disobedient to* *parents, ungrateful, unholy, unloving, irreconcilable, malicious gossips, without self-control, brutal, haters of good, treacherous, reckless, conceited, lovers of pleasure rather than lovers of God, holding to a form of godliness, although they have denied its power…"* 2 Timothy 3:1-5

DO *"…point these things out to the brothers and sisters, and you will be a **good minister** of Christ Jesus, **nourished on the truths of the faith** and of the **good teaching** that you have followed."* 1 Timothy 4:6 (NIV)

DO *"**Encourage one another,** and even more as you see the day approaching."* Hebrews 10:25

DO *"Watch your life and doctrine closely. Persevere in them…"* 1 Timothy 4:16 (NIV)

DO *"…eagerly await Him."* Hebrews 9:28

DO *"…remember the words spoken beforehand by the holy prophets and the commandment of the Lord and Savior spoken by your Apostles."* 2 Peter 3:2

DO *"Set your mind on the things above, not on the things that are on earth."* Colossians 3:2

DO *"Consider how to stimulate one another to love and good deeds."* Hebrews 10:24

DO *"Grow in the grace and knowledge of our Lord and Savior Jesus Christ."* 2 Peter 3:18

BE *"Be the sort of people you ought to be in **holy conduct** and **godliness**, looking for and hastening the coming of the day of God."* 2 Peter 3:11

BE *"Be diligent to be found by Him **in peace, spotless and blameless**, and regard the patience of our Lord as salvation..."* 2 Peter 3:14

BE *"Be on your guard so that **you are not carried away by the error of unprincipled men** and **fall from your own steadfastness...**"* 2 Peter 3:17

Check 1, 2, 3, Is this thing on?

In our final segment of Part One: the Divine Timeline, we come to an interesting ending which is really the beginning of the end.

(I so want to put a smile emoji right here)

In Revelation 5, the Apostle John is shown a scroll sealed with seven seals. A mighty angel in heaven proclaimed with a loud voice, *"Who is worthy to break the seals and open the scroll?"* But no one in heaven or on earth or under the earth was worthy to break the seals. John began to weep because *"No one was worthy to open the scroll."*

One day I asked God, *"Lord, why is this such a big deal if the seals are not opened?"* I believe He gave me an answer (loosely translated), *"If the seals are not broken, then the end cannot begin. And if the end does not begin, then the days would become so wicked that no one would be saved, and all of humanity would be lost."* (Yikes!)

In Revelation 5:5, one of the Elders in heaven spoke to John and said, **"Do not weep! See, the Lion of the tribe of Judah, the Root of David, has triumphed. He is able to open the scroll and its seven seals."** (NIV) This worthy One, AKA Jesus, is the only One who could and did pay humanity's wage of sin, which is death. And because He sacrificed Himself for us, only He is worthy to bring an end to our sin by breaking the seals, thereby judging and destroying the sinful fallen state of humanity once and for all. And all of this is to ultimately usher in a brand new world where sin is no more forever.

And with that, let's finish Part One with a possible answer to this question, *"How close are we to the breaking of the first seal?"*

The Holy Sound Check

For many years, my husband and I have owned a sound company. For those who aren't quite sure what a "sound company" is, I'll give you a short explanation. In its most basic form, it's a business that provides speakers, microphones, and equipment to amplify bands for medium to large, indoor or outdoor, live concerts & festivals. We also sometimes worked with a stage company, so we provided a stage, sound, and lighting at the venue as well.

The sound and stage company is always the first to get there hours before the show starts to set up the system. After setting up, the last thing the sound company does before the concert begins is to **check** the system to see if all of the equipment is working correctly. This is called a "sound check." The band will play to get all of the levels right. After the "sound check," it is usually just a few hours before the show officially starts.

If you've ever heard people check a microphone, it might have sounded like this, "Testing 1 2 3, Testing 1 2 3" or "Check 1 2 3, Check 1 2 3" These are universal "mic check" phrases.

After the sound check, there will be time for the band to relax, get dressed, and get ready to go on stage as the people file into the concert area. When it's time, everything will be set for the band. They walk on stage, and the show begins.

A small group of us have been studying the Book of Revelation for the past 2 1/2 years. We are seeing many signs of "the end" popping up especially as it pertains to Israel.

As we see in the Book of Revelation, and in the Book of Daniel, in the final seven years, there will be a third Jewish Temple built in Jerusalem. The Anti-Christ will make a seven-year covenant (agreement) with the Jewish people and he will trick the whole world into following him. But in the middle of the seven years, he will break the agreement, go into the Temple, and declare *himself* to be god. (Daniel 9:27 and 2 Thessalonians 2)

At this time, Revelation chapter 13 tells us that there will be a "mark of the beast" given to all of the people on planet Earth. Those who refuse the mark will be killed. With this "mark," people will be able to buy and sell. But that won't be why they take the "mark of the beast." The Bible says that the main reason they will take it is to "worship" the beast. Wow, how creepy is that? Many, if not all, of these people who were opposed to "religion" and the idea of God-any god, will now, with their whole hearts, worship the devil. This phenomenon is what is called, "the great delusion." (2 Thessalonians 2:11)

Also, according to the Bible, once a person "takes the mark," there will be no hope for them. (Revelation 14:10-11)
People have been saying "The end is near!" since Jesus preached that message 2000 years ago, but clearly, we have

never been so close to the end as we are today. There are several reasons why I believe this, but suffice it to say, *almost everything is in place for the third Jewish Temple to be built in the next few years, if not sooner. (*see **templeinstitute.org**)

Recently, I saw something very interesting on Facebook. An incredibly clever person has figured out that the very last day of 2023 is 12.31.23. If you take away the dots, you have 123123.

When I saw that, I knew it meant that the **"divine sound check"** was about to start. As we walk into 2024, we have been given a program for the "Concert of the Ages" through the Book of Revelation. We have only to read that book to see exactly what's ahead.

On December 31, 2023, the stage will be set, and the Holy Sound Check will commence, "Check 1 2 3, Check 1 2 3." After that, all that's left to do is to wait for the show to begin.

Are you ready? If not, please go to a place by yourself, and sincerely ask Jesus to show you if He's real. He gives to everyone who asks. If you seek Him, He will let you find Him.

Part Two: the Divine End of Time

(After the first seal is broken)

Chapter 3: The seven-year Tribulation begins

(Before beginning Part Two, please revisit **"But First, Jesus"** on page 10)

"I watched as the Lamb opened the first of the seven seals. Then I heard one of the four living creatures say in a voice like thunder, 'Come!' I looked, and there was a white horse. Its rider held a bow; a crown was given to him, and he went out as a conqueror in order to conquer." Revelation 6:1-2 (NIV)

Fellow believers, at first, we may not even know when the first seal has been broken, but as the others are opened, and we get closer to the blowing of the trumpets, it will become painfully obvious that we have, indeed, entered into the final years. So, as we enter these days of the Tribulation, and taking into account that our relationship with Jesus is current, daily, and close, let these four foundational truths be burned into our minds: that **our mission, our mission field, our message, and our mandate have not and will not change.** No matter what happens from this point on, until we breathe our last breath, let us not forget why we are (still) here, and let's testify of the love, power, and salvation of God through Jesus alone! *We are going to the City of God, but we're not there yet. We have a mission to accomplish.*

- **Our MISSION** — **"Isaiah 61"** has not changed just because the first seal has been broken. *"The Spirit of the sovereign Lord is upon me, because He has anointed me to preach good news to the poor; He has sent me to bind up the brokenhearted, to proclaim liberty to the captives, and the freedom to prisoners of darkness; to proclaim the year of the Lord's favor, and the day of vengeance of our God...."* Isaiah 61:1-2a

- **Our MISSION FIELD** — **"the world"** has not changed just because we have only seven years left of humanity. In fact, we should preach to everyone with great urgency, passion and fear for their eternal souls. Our mission field is wherever we are. This is the place, and now is the time. We need to open our mouths to everyone around us warning them of what's coming and sharing with them the only true solution — Jesus.

- **Our MESSAGE** — **"the Gospel"** has not changed just because it seems that lies are prevailing. *"For I delivered to you as of first importance what I also received: that Christ died for our sins in accordance with the Scriptures, that he was buried, that he was raised on the third day in accordance with the Scriptures..."* 1 Corinthians 15:3-4 (ESV) Let's be bold about this Good News and not ashamed of it. *"For I am not ashamed of the gospel, for it is the power of God for salvation to everyone who believes, to the Jew first and also to the Greek."* Romans 1:16

o **Our MANDATE** — **"to preach the Gospel and to make disciples"** has not changed just because we are being persecuted. On the contrary, let us preach this "Good News" of the truth of Jesus with even more fervor than ever before! The darker the night, the more the light will cut through that darkness with truth and life. *"... holding fast to the word of life..."* Philippians 2:16 Let the testimony of Jesus always be on our lips!

In the midst of difficult times: Remember

*But realize this, that in **the last days** difficult times will come."* 2 Timothy 3:1

"But the Advocate, the Holy Spirit, whom the Father will send in my name, will teach you all things and will remind you of everything I have said to you." John 14:26 (NIV)

John the Baptist: John knew for sure that Jesus was the One. God had told him what to look for as he was baptizing. Sure enough, Jesus came along, and John knew, even as He was coming toward him to be baptized by him, John said, *'Behold, the Lamb of God Who takes away the* *sin of the world!"* John 1:29 (ESV) Then, when John saw the dove landing on Jesus' head and remaining there, that's when it was locked in for him. Jesus was the Messiah, and no one was going to convince him otherwise; that is, until.... John finds himself in prison for preaching a message of righteousness to Herod (Mark 6:18). While he was in jail, he started to doubt whether Jesus was the Anointed One. So, he sent a message to Jesus, *"Are You the One who is to come, or should we look for another?"* Matthew 11:2 (ESV)

And what did Jesus reply? Please listen carefully.
"Go and tell John what you hear and see: the blind receive their sight and the lame walk, lepers are cleansed and the deaf hear, and the dead are raised up, and the poor have good news preached to them. And blessed is the one who is not offended by me." Matthew 11:4-6 (ESV)

What had John forgotten? He forgot the word that God had clearly spoken to him. He forgot that Jesus was the miracle worker. In his fear, John had begun to listen to the wrong voice. When this happens to us (and it does, and will), we need to **remember** the times that we have heard from God. Hearing from God could look like having a dream, an answered prayer, or remembering the day we met Jesus when He saved us. And let's **remember** all of the promises that are written for us in the Scriptures, too. Our lives are chock-full of promises from God! We just have to **remember** them. The enemy is hoping that we will forget that God will always keep His promises. When everything goes haywire, the enemy is banking on us forgetting that God is good ALL the time, and ALL the time, God is good. But if we **remember** the faithfulness of God, the goodness of God, the love of God, and the sovereignty of God, when things get murky, we will have clarity, and we will trust God all the more. Because God, the Holy Spirit lives in us and works within us to remind us of how totally awesome He is!

Remember that God is Sovereign - He rules over all.

Remember that God is omnipotent - He is all-powerful.

Remember that God is Omniscient - He knows all.

Remember that God is Omnipresent - He is everywhere.

Remember that God is with us, He loves us, He's for us, He's interceding for us, He will never leave us, or forsake us, or disown us. Our God is real and present in our midst right now. We have nothing to fear; not the devil, nor people, nor the governments or authorities of this world. We are safe and sound in the arms of our God. "*...where does my help come from? My help comes from the Lord, the Maker of heaven and earth.*" Psalm 121:1b-2 (NIV)

Remain Calm & Trust Jesus

We serve the same God as the disciples, but not in the same "times." We are at the "end of time," and that makes all the difference as to what we can expect as far as trials go. Having said that, we need to approach this Tribulation in the same way as they did, and that is by FAITH in all of

God's promises. Our faith is a weapon, and our faith is what overcomes the world! *"For whatever is born of God overcomes the world; and this is the victory that has overcome the world—our faith. Who is the one who overcomes the world, but he who believes that Jesus is the Son of God?"* 1 John 5:4-5 (NASB)

The Blessing of the Book of Revelation

It's all in the Plan

*"**The Revelation of Jesus Christ**, which God gave Him to show to His bond-servants, the things which must soon take place; and He sent and communicated it by His angel to His bond-servant John, who testified to the word of God and to the testimony of Jesus Christ, everything that he saw. **Blessed is the one who reads, and those who hear the words of the prophecy and keep the things** which are written in it; **for the time is near.**" Revelation 1:1-3*

"Revelation" means "unveiling." So, the Book of the Revelation of Jesus Christ was written for the expressed purpose of "Unveiling Jesus Christ." It's truly an amazing book that was specifically meant to remind the "last days' believers" (us) that God has a plan, and that HE is on the throne even in the midst of the worst time in human history. This Book is a gift — a blessing that God wrote down for us so that we could know Who's coming and what's coming in order to navigate (with courage and confidence) our way through the Tribulation.

I love how God chose John, the youngest of the disciples (during Jesus' ministry on earth), and the only one remaining of the official twelve Apostles by the time of the writing of the Book of Revelation. The other disciples had all been martyred for their faith. Thus, fulfilling what Jesus had said to Peter after His rising from the dead, *"Jesus answered, 'If I want him (John) to remain alive until I return, what is that to you? You must follow me.'"* (John 21:22 NIV) "You follow Me." That's a good Word for us as well, as we try not to compare ourselves to others in the Body, or project onto others when we are being corrected by God.

"I, John, your brother and fellow partaker in the tribulation and kingdom and perseverance which are in Jesus, was on the island called Patmos because of the word of God and the testimony of Jesus." Revelation 1:9

John, 'the disciple whom Jesus loved', was about 95 years old when he penned these words. He had just been banished to an island for criminals because he had been testifying of Jesus. Tradition says that before he was sent to the Isle of Patmos, they tried to kill John by boiling him in a cauldron of oil! Now, we can reasonably assume that this mode of execution was effective to cause the death in everyone else in the past, but not John. In fact, "Tradition" also says that John was not killed by this, but that John was completely unharmed by the attempt! Some say that the Romans would carry out such executions publicly in the Roman Colosseum. If that's true, can you imagine the people who witnessed this? You would have to be a certain kind of person to buy tickets to see this type of thing, then only to witness a miracle of God! I'm sure it changed many people forever, and that testimony should help to build our faith as well.

You see, our God is the sovereign ruler over the realm of mankind, and He is in charge of the number of days that each of us has. God wasn't finished with ninety-five year old John. God had more work to do through him, and He could trust him to do it. John could have given up right here, and no one would've blamed him. But that's not what John did. God sent the 'message of all messages' to John 2000 years ago in order to show **us** today, at least a couple of things: One, that Jesus is the King of all kings-there's no one higher than Him — He is God, and two, that God has a plan for us and for the end that cannot be changed or altered in any way — God is in total control of everything that happens. He is seated on the throne.

Of course we know this is true (in our heads anyway), but when we get to the middle of the seven year Tribulation (3 1/2 year mark), we're going to really need to believe this with our whole heart. Because knowing these truths of God, and seeing with the eyes of faith now will help us to continue to fix our eyes on Jesus when nothing seems to make sense around us during the Seals and the Trumpets.

At this point, I want to encourage all of us not to give up. Let's not grow weary in our contending (fighting) for the Faith. (Jude 2) It's getting hard to breathe, I know, but we have to hold fast to Jesus Who is the Word of Life. This will all be over soon, and we will be with the Lord forever. If John could be obedient in the midst of his great suffering, then so can we!

John didn't write this book for himself. He wrote it down for the last days' believers—I believe that the Book of Revelation was written to us and for us. I so appreciate John for not giving up. He served the Lord faithfully all the way to the end, and we are the recipients of the blessing of **his obedience.** Let's follow his example of perseverance and obedience to what God tells us to do in these last moments.

"Blessed is the one who reads aloud the words of this prophecy, and blessed are those who hear and obey what is written in it, because the time is near." Revelation 1:3 (BSB) After studying the Revelation of Jesus Christ for many years, I can honestly say that I am indeed blessed, first, to see more of Who Jesus really is. This is such a beautiful thing! And second, to know that (in many ways) I won't be surprised by what's coming. *I think we can all agree that it's better to know and be prepared than not to know and be taken by surprise.*

What does "being prepared" look like? Well, I think it looks a lot like giving attention to what God has already shown us, and to wholeheartedly believe it. It helps me to know that all of this is not some random act of chaos driven and controlled by the devil. That kind of thinking is a lie that makes me feel helpless. As a general rule, we as humans, feel better when there is a plan because a plan brings order, and order brings us peace.

Speaking of the Plan...

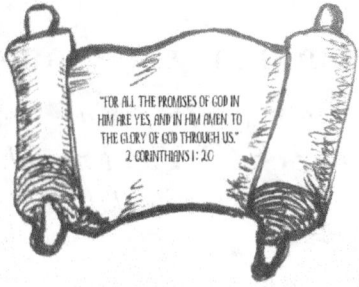

"The Old Testament, written hundreds of years before Jesus' birth, contains over 300 prophecies that Jesus fulfilled through His life, death and resurrection. Mathematically speaking the odds of anyone fulfilling only **eight** prophecies is 1 in 100,000,000,000,000,000 (one hundred quadrillion)." (CBN.com)

(See this link for some of the prophesies that
Jesus fulfilled during His life, death and resurrection:)
https://www2.cbn.com/article/prophecy/biblical-prophecies-fulfilled-jesus"

If God was faithful to keep His word back then, why wouldn't He keep His word now?

Just as there was a plan to redeem mankind from before the creation of the world, there is also a plan for the end of this time as we know it. This plan extends, of course, throughout all eternity. There's no need to worry. God is on His Throne, and He has EVERYTHING under control, including, but not limited to the timing of THE PLAN.

Timing is everything

*"'And the four angels, who **had been prepared for the hour and day and month and year,** were released, so that they would kill a third of mankind*." Revelation 9:15

Do you see what I see?
These are a couple of horrifying verses, to be sure, but what I see here is the absolute sovereign plan of God in action. The angels "...***had been prepared for the hour and day and month and year....***" God has each minute detail planned out to the hour, the day, the month and the year. Not one hour before or after, not one day later, not the seventh month if He planned it for the second month, and not a year too soon or too late. This is just *one example* of the **FACT** that God has everything under control. Right now, at this very moment, it may not look like He does, but rest assured, we are on the winning side even if it looks like we're losing. *It's all in the plan. Never forget that.*

The Fourth Seal — Death

Remain Calm & Trust Jesus.

"When the Lamb broke the fourth seal, I heard the voice of the fourth living creature saying, 'Come.' I looked, and behold, an ashen horse; and he who sat on it had the name Death, and Hades was following with him. Authority was given to them over a fourth of the earth, to kill with sword and with famine and with pestilence and by the wild beasts of the earth." Revelation 6:7-8

If Jesus has opened this seal, there is so much death that we don't have time to grieve the loss of one before another death is upon us. According to the Scripture above, we are seeing "bulk death." This must be similar to wartime loss of life, but still staggeringly more. Death is our enemy, and it always will be until it is thrown into the Lake of Fire along with **Hell** (see Revelation 20:14). Life was never meant to include death. It was never meant to be like this, but because of sin, Death exists. It's the wage of our sin. It's what we deserve as payment for our short-lived, "fun for a time," sin-filled behavior, and it demands something (or someone) to die. These Seals and Trumpets are just the tip of the iceberg of the judgment of God upon the wicked sinfulness of humanity. And we are here because *God can trust us* to **remain calm and trust Him**.

*Oh, God, help us not to become calloused to the loss of life during this time. Help us to remain "human," showing compassion to the lost, boldly telling them the Good News of Your Kingdom, without one thought to our own lives because we have already died and our lives are hidden in You. (Colossians 3) Lord, let us not get used to the smell of death, or the reports of the dying. Help us not to blame You, or question You as You have already warned us that this was coming. But it's so hard right now to see this devastation. It's a small taste of what You have experienced because of us since the beginning of creation. God, please forgive us for offending You, and we beg for Your mercy for those who don't know You. Still, we rejoice in You today, Lord God, Creator, Redeemer, our Refuge, our Rock, our strong tower, our beautiful Savior, our merciful and gracious King. You are worthy of all of our service, our worship, and adoration, both now and forevermore. Dear Jesus, thank You for Your mercy and Your grace that has saved us! Thank You for trusting us to weather the storm of this Tribulation. You have trusted Your followers to be strong in the power of **Your** might. You know that we will not fail You because You are going to make sure that we will stand strong, hold on, and hold fast to You as if our life depended on You because it does. Be glorified, Adonai, Yeshua. Be worshipped and adored every day and in every circumstance. Even through cracking and labored voices, we whisper a song of our love for You, as we celebrate Your goodness, and Your love for us. "I love You Lord, and I lift my voice to worship You, Oh, my soul, rejoice. Take joy my King in what You hear. May it be a sweet, sweet sound in Your ear."* ("I Love You Lord" by Laurie Klein 1978)

Reasons to Rejoice

"Rejoice in the Lord always: and again I say, Rejoice."
Philippians 4:4

When something is *that* important, sometimes you have to say it twice. But how can we rejoice in the Lord when everything is so bad? Keep in mind that the Apostle Paul was in jail for his testimony of Jesus when he wrote to the Philippians.

It's natural for people who are suffering to be sad, but the children of God are not natural, we are supernatural! No matter what the circumstances, we *can* rejoice. We *must* rejoice in the Lord. Here are just a few reasons to rejoice:

- *"This is the day which the LORD has made; Let us rejoice and be glad in it."* Psalm 118:24 Keep in mind that this verse is following the prophesy of Jesus being crucified. ("The Stone which the builders rejected has become the chief Cornerstone." Psalm 118:22)

- *"Nevertheless do not rejoice in this, that the spirits are subject to you, but rejoice that your names are recorded in heaven."* Luke 10:20 Oh, I love this one so much! As these days progress, we can rejoice that our destiny and destination is secured for us in heaven. Jesus was able to go to the cross for that same joy that was set before Him. He came from heaven to accomplish the mission of saving the world, and He was able to endure the suffering by focusing on heaven. (See Hebrews 12:2)

We can do anything if we know who we are, whose we are, and where we're going!

- *"Rejoice greatly, O daughter of Zion! Shout in triumph, O daughter of Jerusalem! Behold, your king is coming to you; He is just and endowed with salvation, Humble, and mounted on a donkey, even on a colt, the foal of a donkey."* Zechariah 9:9 This verse has been fulfilled, but our King *is* coming back for us, and this time He will be on a white horse, and we will be with Him! (See Revelation 19:11-16). **Soon and very soon, we are going to see the King!**

- **How often should we rejoice?** *"Rejoice ALWAYS...."* 1 Thessalonians 5:16

  Even in the bad times? Yup. Even in the sad times? Yup. Even the in-between times? Yup. Even in The Tribulation times? Yup.
  Always. Rejoice.

Remaining Humble, Thankful & Prayerful

Thankfulness to God is what true humility looks like.

Without thanksgiving to God, we can't even get into the door of His presence!

Remaining Humble

- *"Enter His gates with thanksgiving and His courts with praise; give thanks to Him and praise His name. For the Lord is good and His love endures forever; His faithfulness continues through all generations."* Psalm 100:4-5 (NIV) Thanksgiving is the entry point to God's presence because gratitude is the expression of a humble heart. And I'm convinced that humility is one of the most beautiful things to God. Jesus loves, loves, loves it when we give Him thanks! I've never seen a prideful person who's thankful, or a humble person who's not filled with gratitude. It's like the law of gravity. *"God is opposed to the proud, but He gives grace to the humble."* James 4:6

Remaining Thankful

- *"...in everything give thanks; for this is the will of God for you in Christ Jesus."* 1 Thessalonians 5:18

How many things should we be thankful for? Fifty percent of things? Ninety-nine percent of things? Only the things that seem fair and just? No. We need to be thankful in one hundred percent of things — *'in everything give thanks because this is what God wants.'* No matter where we are in the "Divine Timeline," we can practice being pleasing to the Lord by being **thankful in everything**.

- *"...always giving thanks to God the Father for everything in the name of our Lord Jesus Christ."* Ephesians 5:20

How often should we give thanks? **Always, in and for everything!**

Remaining Prayerful

- *"Rejoice always; **pray without ceasing**…."*
  1 Thessalonians 5:16-17

- *"Do not be anxious about anything, but in every situation, by prayer and petition, with thanksgiving, present your requests to God."* Philippians 4:6 *(NIV)*

- *"**Watch and pray** so that you will not fall into temptation. The spirit is willing, but the flesh is weak."* Matthew 26:41 *(NIV)*

- *"Therefore confess your sins to each other and **pray for each other** so that you may be healed. The prayer of a righteous person is powerful and effective." James 5:16 (NIV)*

- *Jesus said, "And whatever **you ask** in My name, this I will do, so that the Father may be glorified in the Son. If **you ask Me** anything in My name, I will do it."* John 14:13-14

- *"With all **prayer and petition pray** [with specific requests] at all times [on every occasion and in every season] in the Spirit, and with this in view, stay alert with all perseverance and petition [interceding in prayer] for all God's people."* Ephesians 6:18 (Amp)

There you have it. If we pray to God all the time, we will find relief from anxiety. When we are alert in prayer, we won't enter into temptation. When we pray for one another, we can be healed because Jesus' blood makes us righteous and therefore, our prayers are effective! And it's totally amazing that Jesus gave us a blank check for whatever we need from Him. Whatever we ask for that glorifies God, He will give it to us. And Ephesians 6:18 sums it all up (Please read that again).

Sisters and brothers, we will not make it through this terrible time with any kind of peace if we are not humble, thankful and in constant prayer to God. Any good relationship consists of two things: communication and presence. Let's be sure to guard our time with God as we seek to grow ever closer to our Savior and Lord, Jesus Christ. We'll simply never make it otherwise.

Staying Together

In a world that's falling apart

*"Let us **hold fast** the confession of our hope without wavering, for **He who promised is faithful;** and let us consider how to **stimulate one another to love and good deeds**, not **forsaking our own assembling together**, as is the habit of some, **but encouraging one another;** and **all the more as you see the day drawing near.**"* Hebrews 10:23-25

If we're not gathering, we're scattering. And if we're scattering, we're losing. For the Body of Christ, we're never called to "divide and conquer." If we divide, we will be conquered. Rather, we are called to "Unite and Overcome!"

Jesus will get us through this, but it comes down to *how* we get through it. We are the Body of Christ, and members of one another. We **cannot** make it on our own without our sisters and brothers helping us. If we try, we will fail. We have not yet reached the mid-point of this Tribulation, so we "ain't seen nothin yet" as far as trouble goes. If you're not gathering with the saints more and more, then you're going to be missing a measure of **strength training** that will make the part that's coming that much harder to navigate.

The true bond of fellowship is actually fostered during the hardest, most stressful times. When people suffer together, they get stronger together. Think about soldiers in a battle. When they make it through, there is a forever bond between them. Why? Because they faced death together. They trusted each other to have their back, and they were willing to lay down their lives for each other. Jesus said there is no greater love than a person laying down their life for a friend, and Jesus modeled this for us on the cross. Very soon, all of us as believers will be under threat of persecution and death if we're not there already. Let's not forsake our assembling together. We need one another in order to "...*hold fast our confession of our hope without wavering....*" *(Hebrews 10:23)* and we desperately need the encouragement of our sisters and brothers in Christ as we step into these final minutes of the last hour of these last days. We need to love one another as Jesus loved us and gave Himself for us. This is a love that the world can never have because God is love, and if a person doesn't have God, they don't have true love. Celebrate the smallest victories together with worship and thanksgiving to God. Whether for a moment or as much time as possible. Our time together may be in secret, and it may be quiet or even sometimes in silence, but we must find a sister or brother at every opportunity to receive the strength, second-wind, and courage, that we all desperately need right now. Fellowship with — getting into the presence of other believers is like oxygen, and we all need oxygen to live well through this time of trouble.

Witness Means Martyr

"I face death every day—yes, just as surely as I boast about you in Christ Jesus our Lord." Paul, the Apostle, 1 Corinthians 15:31 (NIV)

When we said **"yes"** to Jesus, we said **yes** to everything He was offering. Of course, we didn't necessarily understand all that we were saying **yes** to, but in every believer's heart there is necessarily present a **"surrendering all"** in our initial desperate cry for help and salvation. Thankfully, our awesome God does not require us to figure it all out. Instead, Jesus has given us everything we need to live a godly life and to overcome. And we are equipped right now for this victory!

Jesus is speaking to His disciples (and that includes us!), *"...but you will receive power when the Holy Spirit has come upon you; and you shall be My witnesses...." Acts 1:8*

What will we receive when the Holy Spirit has come upon us? **Power,** which in the Greek is, **"dunamis"**, from which we get our English word, *dynamite*. That power is also *"miraculous power."* What is the only reason mentioned by Jesus for giving us such miraculous, dynamite power? He's giving us the power to be **His witnesses.** Interestingly, the word, *"witness"* in the Greek language is, **"martus."** It's where we get our word, *"martyr."*

Let's recap. Jesus, Himself has empowered us through God, the Holy Spirit, to **"be ...His (witnesses) martyrs."** Jesus is saying that the Holy Spirit will, with miraculous, dynamite power, **give us the ability** not only to **live for Jesus** but also *to die for Him!*

We will give more encouragement regarding "martyrs" in chapter 5 as we experience the "middle of the week" or the 3 1/2 year mark of the seven-year Tribulation. As we near the halfway point, it's going to be unbearable for those without Jesus. But it also means that we, as believers, are just a few months away from our eternal reward. **So hold on. Hold fast to your hope. Be on the alert. Get so close to Jesus that you can feel His breath tangibly in your ear as He says,** *"this is the way, walk in it."* **Stay/cling together with other believers. Preach the Gospel of Jesus. Stand firm, and stay the course.**

Child of God, we have GOD'S miraculous power in order to live as His witnesses or to die as His martyrs. Either way, we win in the end.

Chapter 4: The Middle of the "Week"

(We are @ the 3 1/2 year mark)

*"Then after the sixty-two weeks, the Messiah will be cut off and have nothing, and the people of the prince who is to come will destroy the city and the sanctuary. And its end will come with a flood; even to the end there will be war; desolations are determined. And **he will confirm a covenant with the many for one week, but in the middle of the week he will put a stop to sacrifice and grain offering; and on the wing of abominations will come the one who makes desolate,** until a complete destruction, one that is decreed, gushes forth on the one who makes desolate."* Daniel 9:26-27

(also see Daniel 11:36 "And the king shall do according to his will; and he shall exalt himself, and magnify himself above every god, and shall speak marvelous things against the God of gods, and shall prosper till the indignation be accomplished: for that that is determined shall be done.") It's all in the plan!

The "he" in the bold print in the Scripture above is the "Man of Lawlessness," the "anti-Christ." This is an actual man who is described in detail in many places in the Bible. Suffice it to say, this man is going to appear to the Jewish people to be their long-awaited Messiah, and they will embrace him as such. He will proceed to make a covenant (agreement/contract) with the Jews for seven years (one week). He will help them to build the third Temple on the

Temple Mount in Jerusalem. In this covenant there is an agreement to restore the regular sacrifices. Keep in mind, the Jewish people have not had a Temple for 2000 years since it was destroyed by the Romans in 70 AD. Since there has been no Temple, there have also not been any sacrifices (of animals for the atonement of sin) made. The anti-Christ will break the agreement that he made with them in the middle of the seven years (the middle of the week), and he will go into the most Holy place in the Temple and declare himself to be God. That's when the devil will take the stage in his next to last performance on planet earth. It's at this point that the "man of lawlessness" is revealed and all "H E double hockey sticks" is unleashed. This is where we pick up in 2 Thessalonians 2:1-4

*"Now concerning the coming of our Lord Jesus Christ and our **being gathered to him**: We ask you, brothers and sisters, not to be easily upset or troubled, either by a prophecy or by a message or by a letter supposedly from us, alleging that the **Day of the Lord** has come. Don't let anyone deceive you in any way. For that day **will not come** unless the apostasy comes first and the man of lawlessness is revealed, the man doomed to destruction. He opposes and exalts himself above every so-called god or object of worship, so that he sits in God's temple, proclaiming that he himself is God."* 2 Thessalonians 2:1-4 (CSB)

The way I read this, there are **TWO THINGS** that have to occur before Jesus comes to "gather or catch up" (Rapture) us to Himself. **One** - the *"apostasy," aka, "the great falling*

away," and **two** - the *'man of lawlessness' is revealed."*
Let's look at these two things one at a time.

The Apostasy - the Great Falling Away

In the very end, it's not the prodigals coming home, it's the fake Christians falling away

Apostasy: ἀποστασία apostasía, ap-os-tas-ee'-ah; feminine of the same as; **defection from truth** (properly, **the state**) ("apostasy"):—**falling away, forsake.**

*"But the Spirit explicitly says that **in later times** some will* **fall away from the faith**, *paying attention to deceitful spirits and doctrines of demons…."* 1 Timothy 4:1

*"Then they will deliver you to tribulation, and will kill you, and you will be hated by all nations because of My name. **At that time** **many will fall away** and will betray one another and hate one another. Many false prophets will arise and will mislead many. Because lawlessness is increased, most people's love will grow cold."* Matthew 24:9-11

At this point, I'm going to bring up the passage in Scripture that sparks fear into pretty much every believer, but it doesn't have to.

*"Not everyone who says to me, 'Lord, Lord,' will enter the kingdom of heaven, but only the one who does the will of my Father who is in heaven. **MANY** will say to me on that day, 'Lord, Lord, did we not prophesy in your name and in your name drive out demons and in your name perform many miracles?' **Then** I will tell them plainly, 'I **never** knew **you**. Away from me, you **evildoers!**'"* Matthew 7:21-23

How is this possible? Can we know Jesus, but Him not know us? What He says in verse 21 is telling. *"Only those who **do the will** of my Father will enter the Kingdom of Heaven."* So they come back and say, 'Yeah, but weren't we doing what You wanted us to do by prophesying, casting out demons, and working miracles IN YOUR NAME?' He's like, "Yeah, no. I NEVER knew you, get away from Me, you workers of iniquity." (Oh boy)

Even with all of the good they did in Jesus' name, Jesus is unwelcoming to them, insisting that **"I NEVER KNEW YOU."** Notice He didn't say, "I once knew you, but not anymore." No. They were **never** His children to begin with.

Jesus also said, *"My sheep hear my voice, and **I know them**, and **they follow me**: and I give eternal life to them, and they shall never perish; and no one shall snatch them out of My hand."* John 10:27-28

*"I am the good shepherd, and I **know My own** and My own know Me, **even** as the Father knows Me and I know the Father; and I lay down My life for the sheep"* John 10:14-15

I'm convinced that while a person can be bold in Jesus' name, their holy facade will not stand up to persecution, and certainly not to the kind of suffering that threatens their life. This is where the "great" falling away comes in. You see, either we have a relationship with Jesus or we don't. Either He knows us or He doesn't. Christians may fall down, but never "away." We may have "left our first love" (and we need to get back to Him immediately), but we don't "lose" our first love. That being said, we all need to press in hard to our relationship with Jesus in these last moments before we go to be with Him forever. It's not going to be easy, but He already told us that it wouldn't be. I know it's crazy hard to watch these people whom we thought were "of us," but they are not, and have turned into our enemies. Still, God has equipped us with everything we need not to just barely make it through these times, but we have all we need to **overcome** the world, the flesh, and the devil! Why? Because we have received the *love of the Truth*, and we are saved.

Some of Jesus' last words before going to the cross on the night He was betrayed were, "*I am the Way, the Truth, and the Life. No one comes to the Father except through me.*" John 14:6

Sister and brother in Christ, do you love Jesus? Then you do love the Truth because that's WHO truth is. And if we love Him (the Truth), then we will love His will (what He wants). And if we love His will enough to obey Him, then we are considered His family:

He replied to him, "Who is my mother, and who are my brothers?" Pointing to his disciples, he said, "Here are my mother and my brothers. For whoever does the will of my Father in heaven is my brother and sister and mother." Matthew 12:48-50 (NIV)

"Fake Christians" are the ones who are falling away right now, and there are a lot of them. Notice in the above verses that it says, "many" will fall away? True Christians will never fall away from Jesus (See John 6:39 *"And this is the will of Him who sent Me, that I shall lose none of those He has given Me, but raise them up at the last day." (NIV)* **And** *"...and I give eternal life to them, and they shall never perish; and no one shall snatch them out of My hand."* John 10:28)

If you are unsure of whether Jesus knows you at all, I would urge you to get right with Jesus this very minute. Ask Him to forgive you and to save you. Don't hesitate! Don't put it off! Call upon the name of Jesus and be saved! Because pretty soon, there won't be a choice. What is coming for those who haven't received the Love of the Truth is a "great delusion" that will **make them** follow the lie. In fact, they will be so deceived, that they will gladly swear their allegiance to the **Beast** as they take his mark as an act of worship to **him.** (*"And the whole earth was amazed and followed after the beast...."* Revelation 13:3b)

"...that is, the one whose coming is in accord with the activity of Satan, with all power and false signs and wonders, and with all the deception of wickedness for

*those who perish, because they **did not accept** the **love of the truth** so as to be saved. **For this reason** God will send upon them a deluding influence so that they will believe what is false, in order that they all may be judged who did not believe the truth, but took pleasure in wickedness."*
2 Thessalonians 2:9-12

Remain Calm & Trust God

The Man of Lawlessness Revealed

*"No one is to deceive you in any way! For it (the rapture, the day of the Lord) will not come unless the apostasy comes first, **and the man of lawlessness is revealed, the son of destruction, who opposes and exalts himself above every so-called god or object of worship, so that he takes his seat in the temple of God, displaying himself as being God."** 2 Thessalonians 2:3-4*

As we saw at the beginning of this section, the Book of Daniel is running parallel with the Book of Revelation on many things. Again, God has an ironclad plan, and He is not surprised in the least bit by what is happening. He's the Master Builder of the Plan. That being said, the "saints" are in for a bumpy ride. All of the following verses (written thousands of years ago) pertain to the very time and place that I think we are right now.

Because the anti-Christ has taken center stage, things are going to get very, very difficult for us, saints of God. This is where some disturbing events begin to take place. I don't claim to understand this part, but I will declare my trust in God. It's best to know what's coming. That's the entire reason for this book, and for the Book of Revelation. I'm going to show you a series of Scriptures that are not favorable to us as God's people. Remember to **Remain Calm & Trust God**.

"I kept looking, and that horn was waging war with the saints and overpowering them until the Ancient of Days came, and judgment was passed in favor of the saints of the Highest One, and the time arrived when the saints took possession of the kingdom." Daniel 7:21-22

"Thus he said: 'As for the fourth beast, there shall be a fourth kingdom on earth, which shall be different from all the kingdoms, and it shall devour the whole earth, and trample it down, and break it to pieces.'" Daniel 7:23 (NIV) *"And He shall speak words against the Most High, and __shall wear out the saints__ of the Most High...."* Daniel 7:25a (ESV)

"It was also given to him to make war with the saints and to overcome them, and authority was given to him over every tribe, people, language, and nation." Revelation 13:7

"It was given to him...." This phrase is repeated six times in Revelation 13 regarding what the two beasts or the dragon (the unholy trinity of evil) could do. With Whom does ALL authority originate? All authority originates from God

alone. He is the Author of all "**Author**ity." The devil doesn't have any thing on his own. He can't do ANYTHING without God's expressed permission. The devil is a created angel, and like all of us, he is confined to the will and plan of God. He cannot venture outside of those confines. Everything that is happening right now is going according to the divine Plan. That fact alone can bring a great deal of peace to the heart of the child of God during this dark time. Remember, it's all in the plan. Jesus made the plan, He wrote the plan, He is executing the plan, and He will finish His plan. And the whole time, He's going to take care of His people, and we're going to make it because He's going to make us make it.

"What then shall we say to these things? If God is for us, who is against us? He who did not spare His own Son, but delivered Him over for us all, how will He not also with Him freely give us all things? Who will separate us from the love of Christ? Will tribulation, or distress, or persecution, or famine, or nakedness, or peril, or sword?" Romans 8:31-32, 35

We're going to a city whose builder and maker is God! But first, we need to "overcome" the enemy. How exactly are we going to do that?

We shall overcome!

"And they (the saints) overcame and conquered him (the devil) because of the blood of the Lamb and because of the word of their testimony, for they did not love their life and

renounce their faith even when faced with death." Revelation 12:11 (Amplified Bible emphasis added)

How do we overcome the devil who seems to be overcoming us? By trusting in Jesus, holding fast our confession, and dying for our faith. That's what we have to do, dear brothers and sisters in Christ. We won't take the mark, so we will be killed.

"I saw thrones on which were seated those who had been given authority to judge. And I saw the souls of those who had been beheaded because of their testimony about Jesus and because of the word of God. They had not worshiped the beast or its image and had not received its mark on their foreheads or their hands. They came to life and reigned with Christ a thousand years." Revelation 20:4 (NIV)

Do NOT take the Mark of the Beast!
It can't be undone!

"And he causes all, the small and the great, and the rich and the poor, and the free men and the slaves, to be given a mark on their right hand or on their forehead, and he provides that no one will be able to buy or to sell, except the one who has the mark, either the name of the beast or the number of his name. Here is wisdom. Let him who has understanding calculate the number of the beast, for the

number is that of a man; and his number is six hundred and sixty-six." Revelation 13:16-18

It's not possible for a true child of God to take this mark, but for those who are wavering in their faith, we encourage you to get "sealed by God" by calling out and surrendering to Jesus. Don't get marked by the devil. Both the seal and the mark are permanent.

"Then another angel, a third one, followed them, saying with a loud voice, 'If anyone worships the beast and his image, and receives a mark on his forehead or on his hand, he also will drink of the wine of the wrath of God, which is mixed in full strength in the cup of His anger; and he will be tormented with fire and brimstone in the presence of the holy angels and in the presence of the Lamb. And the smoke of their torment goes up forever and ever; they have no rest day and night, those who worship the beast and his image, and whoever receives the mark of his name.'" Revelation 14:9-11

As a group of us studied this, we found that the "mark" is actually a tattoo of some kind. And taking the "mark of the beast" is an act of worship to the devil, and it CANNOT BE UNDONE! Even if they threaten to kill your child, your mom, or your friend right in front of you, DO NOT take the mark! Please, call on Jesus, and He will help you.

Remember in Acts, chapter 1, Jesus gave us "dynamite power" to live **and** to die for Him. We are His witnesses/ martyrs. He told us that it would probably end this way for us when we signed on to His Kingdom. But remember, death is temporary for the child of God and an immediate trip into the very presence of God! Cling to Jesus. Here's some en"**courage**"ment for us today from those (martyrs) who endured to the end, holding fast to their testimony of Jesus.

Encouragement from the past (martyrs)

"Why would anyone die for a lie?" dh

"Instead, they were longing for a better country, a heavenly one. Therefore God is not ashamed to be called their God, for He has prepared a city for them." Hebrews 11:16 (BSB)

Some Christians may be afraid to die a martyr's death, but we have a great cloud of witnesses that has gone before us to give us the courage, that we would surely have regardless, as the faithfulness and strength of our Lord will abound at the exact time of our need. I pray that the following "last words" and accounts of our fellow brothers and sisters who did not shrink back from their faith in Jesus will utterly wipe away every fear and replace it with courage and resolve. **Don't be afraid, we will make it through this. Jesus will see to it.**

Jesus, as He was *being* crucified for OUR sins — *"But Jesus was saying, 'Father, forgive them; for they do not know what they are doing.'"* Luke 23:34

Stephen as he was *being* stoned him to death — *"Look! I see the heavens opened and the Son of Man standing in the place of honor at God's right hand!... Lord Jesus, receive my spirit. Don't charge them with this sin!"* Acts 7:54-60 (Summary)

Paul, the Apostle — *"For I am already being poured out as a drink offering, and the time of my departure has come. I have fought the good fight, I have finished the course, I have kept the faith; in the future there is reserved for me the crown of righteousness, which the Lord, the righteous Judge, will award to me on that day; and not only to me, but also to all who have loved His appearing."* 2 Timothy 4:6-8

Genesius of Rome – *"There is but one king I know. It is he that I love and worship. If I were to be killed a thousand times for my loyalty to him, I would still be his servant. Christ is on my lips. Christ is in my heart. No amount of suffering will take him from me."* **[https://christianrefuge. org/godly-talk-the-last-words-of-early-church-martyrs/]**

(Genesius suddenly, while performing, had a conversion experience on stage. He announced his new faith, and refused to renounce it, even when ordered to do so by emperor Diocletian. Genesius persisted in his faith, and he was finally ordered to be beheaded.) *wikipedia.org*

Julitta of Caesarea – *"Let the estates I own be ravaged, or given to others. Let me lose my life, and let my body be* *destroyed. Rather that than I should speak one word against you, O Lord, who made me. If they take from me a small portion of this earth and its wealth, I shall exchange it for heaven."*

[https://christianrefuge.org/godly-talk-the-last-words-of-early-church-martyrs/] (The judge demanded that the Christian renounce Christ, for which he promised to return her unlawfully taken property. Julitta resolutely refused the deceitful conditions, and for this she was thrown into a furnace, and burned to death in the year 304.) **[https://www.oca.org/saints/lives/2022/07/31/102155-martyr-julitta-at-caesarea]**

"So we do not lose heart. Though our outer self is wasting away, our inner self is being renewed day by day. For this light momentary affliction is preparing for us an eternal weight of glory beyond all comparison, as we look not to the things that are seen but to the things that are unseen. For the things that are seen are temporary, but the things that are unseen are eternal." 2 Corinthians 4:16-18 (ESV)

From Foxe's Book of Martyrs —

* "Blandina, on the day when she and the three other champions were first brought into the amphitheater, she was suspended on a piece of wood fixed in the ground, and exposed as food for the wild beasts; at which time, by her earnest prayers, she encouraged others. But none of the wild beasts would touch her, so that she was remanded to

prison. When she was again produced for the third and last time, she was accompanied by Ponticus, a youth of fifteen and the constancy of their faith so enraged the multitude, that neither the sex of the one nor the youth of the other were respected, being exposed to all manner of punishments and tortures. Being strengthened by Blandina, he persevered unto death; and she, after enduring all the torments heretofore mentioned, was at length slain by the sword." **(https://books.apple.com/us/book/foxs-book-of-martyrs/id511136937)**

* "The torments were various; and, exclusive of those already mentioned, the martyrs of Lyons were compelled to sit in red-hot iron chairs till their flesh broiled. This was inflicted with peculiar severity on Sanctus, already mentioned, and some others. Some were sewed up in nets, and thrown on the horns of wild bulls; and the carcases of those who died in prison, previous to 'the appointed time of execution,' were thrown to dogs. Indeed, so far did the malice of the pagans proceed that they set guards over the bodies while the beasts were devouring them, lest the friends of the deceased should get them away by stealth; and the offals left by the dogs were ordered to be burnt.'"

"The martyrs of Lyons, according to the best accounts we could obtain, who suffered for the gospel, were forty-eight in number, and their executions happened in the year of Christ 177." (Excerpt From Fox's Book of Martyrs: **(https://books.apple.com/us/book/foxs-book-of-martyrs/id511136937)**

"For here we do not have a permanent city, but we are looking for the city that is to come." Hebrews 13:14 (BSB)

From the Book of Hebrews —the Hall of Faith

"...there were others who were tortured, refusing to be released so that they might gain an even better resurrection. Some faced jeers and flogging, and even chains and imprisonment. They were put to death by stoning; they were sawed in two; they were killed by the sword. They went about in sheepskins and goatskins, destitute, persecuted and mistreated— **the world was not worthy of them.** *They wandered in deserts and mountains, living in caves and in holes in the ground. These were all commended for their faith, yet none of them received what had been promised, since God had planned something better for us so that only together with us would they be made perfect."* Hebrews 11:35b-40 (NIV)

"But in all these things we overwhelmingly conquer through Him who loved us. For I am convinced that neither death, nor life, nor angels, nor principalities, nor things present, nor things to come, nor powers, nor height, nor depth, nor any other created thing, will be able to separate us from the love of God, which is in Christ Jesus our Lord." Romans 8:37-39

Chapter 5: Heaven, Here We Come!

(Ready to Fly!)

Look up, for your redemption draws nigh!

"Listen, I tell you a mystery: We will not all sleep, but we will all be changed— in a flash, in the twinkling of an eye, at the last trumpet. For the trumpet will sound, the dead will be raised imperishable, and we will be changed." 1 Corinthians 15:51-52 (NIV)

"For the Lord Himself will descend from heaven with a shout, with the voice of the archangel and with the trumpet of God, and the dead in Christ will rise first. Then we who are alive and remain will be caught up together with them in the clouds to meet the Lord in the air, and so we shall always be with the Lord. Therefore comfort one another with these words." 1 Thessalonians 4:16-18

*"Then the **seventh angel** sounded; and there were loud voices in heaven, saying, '**The kingdom of the world has become the kingdom of our Lord and of His Christ; and He will reign forever and ever.**' And the twenty-four elders, who sit on their thrones before God, fell on their faces and worshiped God, saying, 'We give You thanks, Lord God, the Almighty, the One who **is** and who **was**, because **You have taken Your great power and have begun to reign.** And the nations were enraged, and Your wrath came, and the time came for the dead to be judged, **and the time to reward Your bond-servants the prophets and the saints and those who fear Your name, the small and the great,** and to destroy those who destroy the earth.'"*
Revelation 11:15-18

When Heaven is finally Our Home

*"Then I saw 'a new heaven and a new earth,' for the first heaven and the first earth had passed away, and there was no longer any sea. I saw the Holy City, the new Jerusalem, coming down out of heaven from God, prepared as a bride beautifully dressed for her husband. And I heard a loud voice from the throne saying, '**Look! God's dwelling place is now among the people, and he will dwell with them. They will be his people, and God himself will be with them and be their God. He will wipe every tear** from their eyes. There will be **no more death or mourning or crying or pain,** for the old order of things has passed away.' He*

who was seated on the throne said, 'I am making everything new!' Then He said, 'Write this down, for these words are trustworthy and true.'" Revelation 21:1-5 (NIV)

"He said to me: 'It is done. I am the Alpha and the Omega, the Beginning and the End. To the thirsty I will give water without cost from the spring of the water of life. Those who are victorious will inherit all this, and I will be their God and they will be My children.'" Revelation 21:6-7 (NIV)

"Then the angel showed me the river of the water of life, as clear as crystal, flowing from the throne of God and of the Lamb down the middle of the great street of the city. On each side of the river stood the tree of life, bearing twelve crops of fruit, yielding its fruit every month. And the leaves of the tree are for the healing of the nations. No longer will there be any curse. The throne of God and of the Lamb will be in the city, and His servants will serve him. They will see His face, and His name will be on their foreheads. There will be no more night. They will not need the light of a lamp or the light of the sun, for the Lord God will give them light. And they will reign for ever and ever.'" Revelation 22:1-5 (NIV)

I Will Dwell in the House of the Lord Forever

"The Lord is my shepherd; I shall want for nothing. He makes me lie down in green pastures. He leads me beside still waters. He restores my soul. He leads me in paths of righteousness for His name's sake. Even though I walk through the valley of the shadow of death, I will fear no evil, for You are with me; Your rod and Your staff, they comfort me. You prepare a table before me in the presence of my enemies; You anoint my head with oil; my cup overflows. Surely, goodness and mercy will follow me all the days of my life, and I will dwell in the House of the Lord forever." Psalm 23 (ESV)

If we should need a signal...

In prior days of persecution, the Christians used the "Christian fish" to show the direction of where they would be meeting in secret.

We can use the Omega sign as a direction for where the saints of God will be meeting.

(NOTE: Arrows are only present on the drawing to show direction. The long line on either side of the dome points to the direction of the meeting.)

It's ALL About Jesus!

"Everything begins and ends with Jesus. He is the beginning and He will bring the end, only to begin anew, to never end again." dh

Jesus is the Creator. He spoke the universe into being, and yet He came to earth as a baby to live a sinless life to pay humanity's debt of sin on the cross. Yes, the first time, He came as a baby, but this time, He's coming back as the King of kings, and Lord of lords to execute the wrath of God, and all of us (His people) will be with Him!

It's fitting to end this handbook with (the unveiled) powerful King Jesus since we began the book with our beautiful Savior, Jesus. There's coming a day when *"...at the name of Jesus every knee will bow, of those who are in heaven, and on earth, and under the earth, and that every tongue will confess that Jesus Christ is Lord, to the glory of God the Father."* Philippians 2:10-11

As you read the following passage aloud, let your faith grow, realizing Who it is that we actually worship, serve, believe and are waiting for. He's gone to prepare a place for us. If it wasn't so, He wouldn't have told us this. Our God is Faithful and True. This is our God:

*"And I saw heaven opened, and behold, a white horse, and He who sat on it is called Faithful and True, and in righteousness He judges and wages war. His eyes are a flame of fire, and on His head are many crowns; and He has a name written on Him which no one knows except Himself. He is clothed with a robe dipped in blood, and His name is called The Word of God. **And the armies which are in heaven, clothed in fine linen,** white and clean, **were following Him on white horses.** From His mouth comes a sharp sword, so that with it He may strike down the nations, and He will rule them with a rod of iron; and He treads the wine press of the fierce wrath of God, the Almighty. And on His robe and on His thigh He has a name written: 'KING OF KINGS, AND LORD OF LORDS.'"* Revelation 19:11-16

"And behold, I am coming quickly, and My reward is with Me, to give to every one according to their work. I am the Alpha and the Omega, the Beginning and the End, the First and the Last." Jesus. Revelation 22:12-13 (NKJ)

I'll see you on the other side.

Your sister in Christ,

Denise

Shalom. Shalom.

Epilogue

We are very close to the end of all things, and Jesus wants you and me to know Him. He did everything possible so that we could be with Him in Heaven for eternity. You see, we are all sinners (we've gravely offended our Creator), and the wages of every and any sin is eternal death. Jesus paid our wage of sin on the cross, and He gave us a gift. But a gift that's unopened is of no benefit at all. Each of us has to come to our own conclusion regarding our need for Jesus. If you realize that you're a sinner in need of a Savior, you can simply call on Jesus to forgive you and save you. As it says in Romans 10:9, *"If you confess with your mouth Jesus is Lord (Master, ruler), and believe in your heart that God raised Him from the dead, you will be saved."* Doing this will begin your relationship with Jesus.

Lest the devil is lying to you at this very moment, please consider these truths that will help you to push back the darkness of those lies.

1. You have not gone too far for God to forgive you and save you right now.

2. You don't have to clean yourself up to come to God. That's God's job.

3. You are worth it! Jesus paid the price for your sin just like He did for all of us.

4. It *IS* that easy. (Because Jesus did all of the work)

Once you begin a genuine relationship with Jesus, you will never be lost again.

The end of all things is near. I believe that **we are the last generation of human beings on this earth as we know it.** I believe in our lifetime, we will see the Book of Revelation come to pass. If I'm wrong, no problem, except that we will all die, and the same thing required for the *"end of time"* is what is required for each one of the *"end of our days."* If I'm right about the timing, then we all need to get ready NOW. I know I'm 100% right that all of us will die, so the decision to follow Jesus is urgent no matter where we are in the "timing" of the end.

Please, don't put it off. Ask Jesus to save you right now. Humbly ask Him to forgive you for offending Him with your sin. Ask Him to cleanse you, and save you. Call out to Jesus and He will rescue you! Accept His gift and live for Him for the rest of your days.

On February 13, 1986, Jesus saved me. I have never looked back, and He has never let me down. If He did it for me, He can do it for you.

If you have questions, please email dhaasbigd@gmail.com and I'll do my best to point you in the direction of Jesus. **Shalom to you, Big D**

Quick Reference Guide Contents:

1   Signs of the Times Checklist

2   The Seven Seals & Trumpets

3   Remember Who Jesus IS

4   The Overcomer's Reward

5   Phrases of Praise (Revelation)

6   Post Script-ures: ('last days' Scriptures)

7   Survey Questions (for witnessing)

Signs of the Times Checklist

Please refer to the Seven Seals & the Seven Trumpets pages for a detailed description of these events

The Seven Seals

☐ **1 Seal:** *Conqueror*

☐ **2 Seal:** *War*

☐ **3 Seal:** *Famine*

☐ **4 Seal:** *Death*

☐ **5 Seal:** *Martyrs under altar*

☐ **6 Seal:** *A great earthquake, sun turns black, moon turns red, stars fall to the earth.*

☐ **7 Seal:** *Silence in heaven 1/2 hour* Ready the 7 Trumpets

The Seven Trumpets

☐ **1 Trumpet:** *Devastation to the earth*

☐ **2 Trumpet:** *Devastation to the sea*

☐ **3 Trumpet:** *Devastation to fresh waters*

☐ **4 Trumpet:** *Sun, moon, stars 1/3 dark*

☐ **5 Trumpet: 1st Woe!** *Abyss is opened*

☐ **6 Trumpet: 2nd Woe!** *Angels at Euphrates released, 1/3 of mankind killed*

☐ **7 Trumpet: 3rd Woe!** The time for God's wrath, judgment, reward for saints, destruction to those who destroy the earth *The kingdom of the world has become the Kingdom of our Lord and He shall reign forever and ever!*

These events will fit in between the Seals and Trumpets *(not necessarily appearing in this order)*

☐ **Man of Peace, AKA the Anti-Christ makes a seven-year covenant with Israel** (This is the first seal being broken. This man is the conqueror [with a crown] He has a bow, but no arrows. He conquers the world.)

☐ The **Temple is built in Jerusalem.** Regular sacrifices are restored.

☐ **Two Witnesses Prophesy in Israel** for 1260 days (3 1/2 years)

☐ **Man of Lawlessness is revealed** *Antichrist breaks the seven-year covenant with Israel in the middle of the seven years (at the 3 1/2 year mark). Goes into the Temple and declares himself to be God.*

☐ **Everyone on the planet must get the Mark of the Beast or be killed.** Persecution and martyrdom of Christians begins.

☐ **The Great Falling Away** *(of false Christians)*

☐ **The Two Witnesses are killed in Jerusalem.** *They leave their dead bodies in the street. Everyone sees it when they rise from the dead 3 1/2 days later. Revelation 11*

☐ **The Last Trumpet sounds - Rapture of the Church** *(the dead in Christ rise, all alive and remain will be gathered together to meet the Lord in the air!)*

What comes after the Church is raptured is the **GREAT** TRIBULATION. This is when God's wrath and the devil's wrath (because he knows his time is short) are POURED out simultaneously upon an unrepentant humanity. Please, please, I beg you to call upon the name of Jesus and ask Him to save you now! Remember John 3:16, *"For God so loved the world (that's you and me) that He gave His Only Son (Jesus/Yeshua) that whoever believes in Him will not perish, but have eternal life."*

The Seven Seals — Revelation 6

1 **The First Seal: Conqueror - white horse**
"… there was a white horse. Its rider held
a bow; a crown was given to him,
and he went out as a conqueror in order
to conquer."
Revelation 6:2 (CSB)

2 **The Second Seal: War - red horse**
"Then another horse came out, a fiery red one.
Its rider was given power to take peace from the
earth and to make people kill each other.
To him was given a large sword."
Revelation 6:4 (NIV)

3 **The Third Seal: Famine - black horse**
"...behold, a black horse, and the one who sat
on it had a pair of scales in his hand.
And I heard *something* like a voice in the center
of the four living creatures saying,
'A quart of wheat for a denarius, and three
quarts of barley for a denarius; and do
not damage the oil and the wine.'"
Revelation 6:5-6

4   **The Fourth Seal: Death - ashen horse**
by sword, famine, plague and wild animals
"...I looked, and behold, an ashen horse; and he who
sat on it had the name Death; and Hades was following
with him. Authority was given to them over a fourth of
the earth, to kill with sword and with famine and with
pestilence and by the wild beasts of the earth."
Revelation 6:8

5   **The Fifth Seal: the martyrs**
"When he opened the fifth seal, I saw under
the altar the souls of those who had been slain because of
the word of God and the testimony they had maintained."
Revelation 6:9 (NIV)

6   **The Sixth Seal**
"I watched as he opened the sixth seal.
There was a great earthquake. The sun turned
black like sackcloth made of goat hair, the whole moon
turned blood red, and the stars in the sky fell to earth, as
figs drop from a fig tree when shaken by a strong wind. The
heavens receded like a scroll being rolled up, and every
mountain and island was removed from its place."
Revelation 6:12-14 (NIV)

7   "When the Lamb broke the seventh seal,
here was silence in heaven for about half
an hour. And I saw the seven angels who stand before
God, and seven trumpets were given to them."
Revelation 8:1-2

The Seven
Trumpets-Revelation 8, 9, 11

1

First Trumpet
"Then the *first angel* sounded his trumpet,
and hail and fire mixed with blood
were hurled down upon the earth. 1/3 of the **earth was
burned up**, along with **1/3 of the trees** and
all the green grass."
Revelation 8:7 (BSB)

2

Second Trumpet
"Then the *second angel* sounded his trumpet,
and something like a great mountain burning
with fire was thrown into the sea. **1/3 of** the
**sea turned to blood, 1/3 of the living creatures in
the sea died**, and **1/3 of** the **ships were destroyed**."
Revelation 8:8-9 (BSB)

3

Third Trumpet
"Then the *third angel* sounded his trumpet,
and a great star burning like a torch fell from heaven
and **landed on 1/3 of the rivers and on the springs** of
water. The name of the star is Wormwood. **1/3 of the
waters turned bitter like wormwood** oil, and many
people died from the bitter waters."
Revelation 8:10-11 (BSB)

4 **Fourth Trumpet**
"Then the *fourth angel* sounded his trumpet,
and 1/3 **of the sun and moon and stars** were struck.
1/3 **of the stars were darkened,** 1/3 of the **day was
without light**, and 1/3 **of the night as well**."
Revelation 8:12 (BSB)

5 **Fifth Trumpet -
Beginning of the "3 Woes"**
"Then the *fifth angel* sounded his trumpet, and I saw a
star that had fallen from heaven to earth, and it was given
the key to the pit of the Abyss. The star opened the pit of
the Abyss, and smoke rose out of it like the smoke of a
great furnace, and the sun and the air were darkened by
the smoke from the pit." *Smoke and locusts came out w/
scorpion stings.* They were permitted to torment for
5 months all who don't have the seal of God.
People will want to die, but won't be able to.
Revelation 9:1-6 (BSB)

6 **Sixth Trumpet**
"Then the *sixth angel* sounded his trumpet,
and I heard a voice from the four horns of the golden
altar before God saying to the sixth angel with the trumpet,
'Release the four angels who are bound at the great river
Euphrates.' So the four angels who had been prepared for
this hour and day and month and year were released to
kill 1/3 of mankind. And the number of mounted troops
was two hundred million...."
Revelation 9:13-16 (BSB)

7   Seventh (LAST) Trumpet

"Then the *seventh angel sounded* his
trumpet and loud voices called out in heaven: 'The
kingdom of the world has become the kingdom
of our Lord and of His Christ, and He will reign
forever and ever.' 'We give thanks to You,
O Lord God Almighty, the One who is and who was,
because You have taken Your great power and
have begun to reign. The nations were enraged, and Your
wrath has come. The time has come to judge the dead and
**to reward Your servants the prophets, as well as the
saints and those who fear Your name, both small and
great** — and to destroy those who destroy the earth.'"
Revelation 11:15, 17-18 (BSB)

Remember Who Jesus IS

This is the way John saw Jesus in the beginning of the Revelation

"And I turned to see the voice that was speaking with me. And having turned I saw seven golden lamp stands; and in the middle of the lamp stands one like a son of man, clothed in a robe reaching to the feet, and girded across His breast with a golden sash. And His head and His hair were white like white wool, like snow; and His eyes were like a flame of fire; and His feet were like burnished bronze, when it has been caused to glow in a furnace, and His voice was like the sound of many waters. And in His right hand He held seven stars; and out of His mouth came a sharp two-edged sword; and His face was like the sun shining in its strength. And when I saw Him, I fell at His feet as a dead man. And He laid His right hand upon me, saying, 'Do not be afraid; I am the first and the last, and the living One; and I was dead, and behold, I am alive forevermore, and I have the keys of death and of Hades.'" Revelation 1:12-18

The following is a collection of the ways that Jesus described Himself to the Seven Churches in chapters 2-3 of The Book of Revelation

◆ *The One Who holds the seven stars (angels) in His right hand... Revelation 2:1*

◆ *The One Who walks among the seven golden lamp stands (Churches)....Revelation 2:1*

◆ *The First and the Last, Who was dead and has come to life...Revelation 2:8*

◆ *The One Who has the sharp two-edged sword... Revelation 2:12*

◆ *The Son of God Who has eyes like a flame of fire, and His feet are like burnished bronze...Revelation 2:18*

◆ *The One Who has (or holds) the seven spirits of God, and the seven stars (angels)...Revelation 3:1a*

◆ *He Who is holy...Revelation 3:18*

◆ *Who is true...Revelation 3:18*

◆ *Who has the Key of David...Revelation 3:18*

◆ *Who opens and no one shuts, and Who shuts and no one will open...Revelation 3:18*

◆ *The Amen...Revelation 3:14*

◆ *The faithful and true Witness...Revelation 3:14*

◆ *The ruler of God's creation...Revelation 3:14*

(See Revelation 19 on page 96)

Jesus is the Great I AM. There is no one like Him, or beside Him, or before Him or after Him. He is the Good Shepherd, and we are His sheep. He will never let us down. He will never abandon us. We have nothing to fear. He is faithful and true and is coming back for us soon, and we will always be with the Lord.

The Overcomer's Reward

Jesus promised rewards to the Church for those who overcome what's coming.

To the one who overcomes:

◆ **I WILL** grant to eat of the tree of life which is in the paradise of God... Revelation 2:7

◆ **I WILL** give you the crown of life, and you shall not be hurt by the second death. (If you are faithful unto death)... Revelation 2:10b, 11b

◆ **I WILL** give you some of the hidden manna, and a white stone, and a new name written on the stone which no one knows but the one who receives it...Revelation 2:17

◆ **I WILL** give you authority over the nations...Revelation 2:26

◆ **I WILL** give you the morning star...Revelation 2:28

◆ **You WILL** be clothed in white garments, and walk with Me...Revelation 3:4

◆ **I WILL NOT** erase your name from the Book of Life... Revelation 3:5

◆ **I WILL** confess your name before My Father... Revelation 3:5

◆ **I WILL** make you a pillar in the House of my God. You will not go out from it anymore forever... Revelation 3:12

◆ **I WILL** write on you the name of My God, the name of the City of My God, and My new name... Revelation 3:12

◆ **I WILL** give the one who overcomes the right to sit with Me on My throne, just as I overcame and have sat down with My Father on His Throne... Revelation 3:12

Phrases of Praise

(from The Book of Revelation)

Revelation 4:8

"And the four living creatures, each one of them having six wings, are full of eyes around and within; and day and night they do not cease to say, 'Holy, holy, holy is the Lord God, the Almighty, Who was and Who is and Who is to come.'"

Revelation 4:10-**11**

"And when the living creatures give glory, honor, and thanks to Him who sits on the throne, to Him who lives forever and ever, the twenty-four elders will fall down before Him who sits on the throne, and they will worship Him who lives forever and ever, and will cast their crowns before the throne, saying, **'Worthy are You, our Lord and our God, to receive glory and honor and power; for You created all things, and because of Your will (Your pleasure) they existed, and were created.'"**

Revelation 5:8-10

"When He had taken the scroll, the four living creatures and the twenty-four elders fell down before the Lamb, each one holding a harp and golden bowls full of incense, which are the prayers of the saints. And they *sang a new song, saying,

"Worthy are You to take the scroll and to break its seals; for You were slain, and You purchased people for God with Your blood from every tribe, language, people, and nation. You have made them into a kingdom and priests to our God, and they will reign upon the earth.""

Revelation 5:11-12

"Then I looked, and I heard the voices of many angels around the throne and the living creatures and the elders; and the number of them was myriads of myriads, and thousands of thousands, saying with a loud voice, **"Worthy is the Lamb that was slain to receive power, wealth, wisdom, might, honor, glory, and blessing.""**

Revelation 5:13-14

"And I heard every created thing which is in heaven, or on the earth, or under the earth, or on the sea, and all the things in them, saying, **'To Him who sits on the throne and to the Lamb be the blessing, the honor, the glory, and the dominion forever and ever.'** And the four living creatures were saying, 'Amen.' And the elders fell down and worshiped."

Revelation 7:11-12

"And all the angels were standing around the throne and *around* the elders and the four living creatures; and they fell on their faces before the throne and worshiped God, saying, 'Amen, blessing, glory, wisdom, thanks-

giving, honor, power, and might *belong* to our God forever and ever. Amen.'"

Revelation 11:15

"Then the seventh angel sounded; and there were loud voices in heaven, saying,

'The kingdom of the world has become *the kingdom* of our Lord and of His Christ; and He will reign forever and ever." And the twenty-four elders, who sit on their thrones before God, fell on their faces and worshiped God...'"

Revelation 11:16-18

"We give You thanks, Lord God, the Almighty, the One who is and who was, because You have taken Your great power and have begun to reign. And the nations were enraged, and Your wrath came, and the time *came* for the dead to be judged, and *the time* to reward Your bond-servants the prophets and the saints and those who fear Your name, the small and the great, and to destroy those who destroy the earth."

Revelation 15:3-4

"And I saw *something* like a sea of glass mixed with fire, and those who were victorious over the beast and his image and the number of his name, standing on the sea of glass, holding harps of God. And they sang the song of Moses, the bond-servant of God, and the song of the Lamb, saying, 'Great and marvelous are Your works, Lord God, the

Almighty; Righteous and true are Your ways, King of the nations! Who will not fear You, Lord, and glorify Your name? For You alone are holy; For all the nations will come and worship before You, for Your righteous acts have been revealed.'"

Revelation 19:1-3

"After these things I heard *something* like a loud voice of a great multitude in heaven, saying,

'Hallelujah! Salvation, glory, and power belong to our God, because His judgments are true and righteous; for He has judged the great harlot who was corrupting the earth with her sexual immorality, and He has avenged the blood of His bond-servants on her.' And a second time they said, 'Hallelujah! Her smoke rises forever and ever.' And the twenty-four elders and the four living creatures fell down and worshiped God who sits on the throne, saying, 'Amen. Hallelujah!'"

Revelation 19:5

"And a voice came from the throne, saying,**'Give praise to our God, all you His bond-servants, you who fear Him, the small and the great."** Then I heard *something* like **the voice of a great multitude and like the sound of many waters, and like the sound of mighty peals of thunder, saying, 'Hallelujah! For the Lord our God, the Almighty, reigns.'"**

Post Script-ures
Last Days' Scriptures

*"God, after He spoke long ago to the fathers in the prophets in many portions and in many ways, **in these last days** has spoken to us in His Son, whom He appointed heir of all things, through whom also He made the world."* Hebrews 1:1-2

*"...but this is what was spoken of through the prophet Joel: 'And it shall be in **the last days,'** God says, 'That I will pour forth of My Spirit on all mankind; and your sons and your daughters shall prophesy, and your young shall see visions, and your old shall dream dreams; Even on My bondslaves, both men and women, I will in those days pour forth of My Spirit and they shall prophesy.'"* Acts 2:16-18 & Joel 2:28-29

*"Know this first of all, that **in the last days** mockers will come with their mocking, following after their own lusts, and saying, 'Where is the promise of His coming? For ever since the fathers fell asleep, all continues just as it was from the beginning of creation.'"* 2 Peter 3:3-4

"But you, brothers and sisters, are not in darkness so that this day should surprise you like a thief. You are all children of the light and children of the day. We do not belong to the night or to the darkness. So then, let us not be like others, who are asleep, but let us be awake and sober. For those who sleep, sleep at night, and those who get

drunk, get drunk at night. But since we belong to the day, let us be sober, putting on faith and love as a breastplate, and the hope of salvation as a helmet. For God did not appoint us to suffer wrath but to receive salvation through our Lord Jesus Christ." 1 Thessalonians 5:4-9 (NIV)

"The end of all things is near; therefore, be of sound judgment and sober spirit for the purpose of prayer." 1 Peter 4:7

"But realize this, that in *the last days* difficult times will come" 2 Timothy 3:1

"Now the *Spirit expressly states* that *in later times* some will abandon the faith to follow deceitful spirits and the teachings of demons..." 1 Timothy 4:1 (BSB)

"In *the last times* there will be scoffers who will follow after their own ungodly desires." Jude 1:18 (NIV)

"For *the time will come* when people will not tolerate sound doctrine, but with itching ears they will gather around themselves teachers to suit their own desires." 2 Timothy 4:3 (BSB)

Jesus said, *"But before all these things, they will lay their hands on you and persecute you, turning you over to the synagogues and prisons, bringing you before kings and governors on account of My name. It will lead to an opportunity for your testimony. So make up your minds not* *to prepare beforehand to defend yourselves; for **I will** **provide you eloquence and wisdom** which none of your adversaries will be able to oppose or refute."* Luke 21:12-15

"Remember what I told you: 'A servant is not greater than his master.' If they persecuted me, they will persecute you also…." John 15:20a

Jesus told the disciples (us), You shall be my Witnesses (Witness means martyr)

Inasmuch as the following passages (in context) apply to the Jewish believers in the final days, there are certainly some parts that can be applied and utilized by every believer.

"Be on your guard; for they will deliver you to the courts, and you will be flogged in the synagogues, and you will stand before governors and kings for My sake, as a testimony to them. The gospel must first be preached to all the nations. When they arrest you and hand you over, do not worry beforehand about what you are to say, but say whatever is given you in that hour; for it is not you who speak, but it is the Holy Spirit. Brother will betray brother to death, and a father his child; and children will rise up against parents and have them put to death. You will be hated by all because of My name, but the one who endures to the end, he will be saved." Jesus. Mark 13:9-13

*"…they will lay their hands on you and will persecute you, delivering you to the synagogues and prisons, bringing you before kings and governors for My name's sake. It **will lead***

to an opportunity for your testimony. So make up your minds not to prepare beforehand to defend yourselves; for I will give you utterance and wisdom which none of your opponents will be able to resist or refute. But you will be betrayed even by parents and brothers and relatives and friends, and they will put some of you to death, and you will be hated by all because of My name." Jesus. Luke 21:12-17

"So when you see standing in the holy place 'the abomination of desolation,' described by the prophet Daniel (let the reader understand), then let those who are in Judea flee to the mountains. Let no one on the housetop come down to retrieve anything from his house. And let no one in the field return for his cloak. How miserable those days will be for pregnant and nursing mothers! Pray that your flight will not occur in the winter or on the Sabbath. For at that time there will be great tribulation, unmatched from the beginning of the world until now, and never to be seen again. If those days had not been cut short, nobody would be saved. But for the sake of the elect, those days will be cut short." Matthew 24:15-22 (BSB)

*The passage above (Matthew 24:15-22) is referring to a third of the Jews who will flee to Petra (most likely in Jordan) and will be protected by God for the last 3 1/2 years.

"Now learn this lesson from the fig tree: As soon as its branches become tender and sprout leaves, you know that summer is near. So also, when you see all these things, you will know that He is near, right at the door. Truly I tell you,

this generation will not pass away until all these things have happened. Heaven and earth will pass away, but My words will never pass away." Matthew 24:32-35 (BSB)

"But of that day and hour no one knows, not even the angels of heaven, nor the Son, but the Father alone. 'For the coming of the Son of Man will be just like the days of Noah. For as in those days before the flood they were eating and drinking, marrying and giving in marriage, until the day that Noah entered the ark, and they did not understand until the flood came and took them all away; so will the coming of the Son of Man be. Then there will be two men in the field; one will be taken and one will be left. Two women will be grinding at the mill; one will be taken and one will be left." Matthew 24:36-41

"Therefore be on the alert, for you do not know which day your Lord is coming. But be sure of this, that if the head of the house had known at what time of the night the thief was coming, he would have been on the alert and would not have allowed his house to be broken into. For this reason you also must be ready; for the Son of Man is coming at an hour when you do not think He will." Matthew 24:42-44

Survey Questions

1. What is your first name? _____

(This will help it be more personal. If you know what their name means, you can tell them now)

2. How often do you listen to the news?   **Multiple times a day   once a day   not at all   Source?** _____

3. How does the news make you feel? **a. Comforted   b. Unsafe   c. Angry   d. Fearful   e. Informed**

4. Do you think we are close to the end of the world?   **yes   no   maybe**

5. In what ways have the past two years been especially worse than at other times in history?

a. The problems are worldwide   b. The violence is more brutal and widespread   c. Since 2020, events have occurred that have never before happened in all of human history   d. Technology and knowledge are increasing at an exponential rate. e. All of these   or f. *nothing is different, it's the natural cycle of things*

6. On a scale from 1-10 with 1 being none and 10 being very high, what is your level of peace? _____

7. To what or to whom do you attribute this peace? _____

8. How do current events make you feel? **a. Anxious b. Angry c. Sad. d. Helpless e. All of the above f. Excited**

9. When you get stressed, what are you more likely to do? (Circle as many as apply- number first to last)

*Pray *Watch TV *Read the Bible *Clean something *Call a friend *Go on social media   *other

☐ *Other* _____

10. Do you know what this current Generation is called? Is it **Millennials, Baby Boomers , Gen X, or Gen Z**
    It's interesting that in our country we are at the last letter in **our** alphabet. Generation **Z** has begun.

11. This book is called "The Omega Generation," do you know what Omega means? **Omega means last. It's like our Z in the Greek Alphabet. So, "the Omega Generation: a handbook for last days' believers" is a tool for the last days Christians to use during the final days of history as we lead up to the Tribulation, and if we should go through any part of the Tribulation, this book will help Christians to navigate a faith-filled path all the way to the end.**

12. If we are in the last days, does that bother you? **Yes   No   a little bit   Why or Why not?**

13. How would you describe your relationship with God? a. **Very close   b. somewhat close   c. distant   d. non existent**

14. If Jesus were to come back today, do you feel that you would be prepared or unprepared? _____

15. What qualifies a person to go to heaven? **a. good works   b. I'm not as bad as murderers, etc.**

                              c. Trusting only in the sacrifice Jesus made on the cross.

16. Last question: Would you like to be informed when this book comes out? If so, email address

_____

That concludes our survey. Thank you so much for your time. Your answers have helped immensely.
Please visit theomegageneration.com to purchase the book.

WE ARE THE OMEGA GENERATION

Our God Reigns!
The Ancient of Days & the Way it All Ends

"I kept looking until thrones were set up, and the Ancient of Days took His seat; His garment was white as snow, and the hair of His head like pure wool. His throne was ablaze with flames, its wheels were a burning fire. A river of fire was flowing and coming out from before Him; thousands upon thousands were serving Him, and myriads upon myriads were standing before Him.

The court sat, and the books were opened. Then I kept looking because of the sound of the boastful words which the horn was speaking; I kept looking until the beast was killed, and its body was destroyed and given to the burning fire. As for the rest of the beasts, their dominion was taken away, but an extension of life was granted to them for an appointed period of time.

*I kept looking in the night visions, and behold, with the clouds of heaven One like a Son of Man was coming, and He came up to the Ancient of Days and was presented before Him. And to **Him was given dominion, honor, and a kingdom,** so that all the peoples, nations, and populations of all languages might serve Him.*

His dominion is an everlasting dominion which will not pass away; and His kingdom is one which will not be destroyed." Daniel 7:9-14

WE ARE THE OMEGA GENERATION

Acknowledgements

THE AUTHOR WOULD LIKE TO THANK THE FOLLOWING PEOPLE
FOR THEIR INVALUABLE CONTRIBUTION TO THIS WORK:
ALL OF THE PRAYER WARRIORS,
ALL OF THOSE WHO GAVE FINANCIALLY, AND
TO THOSE WHO GAVE **BOTH** FINANCIALLY AND IN PRAYER.
THANK YOU TO MY EDITOR, MY HUSBAND, FRIENDS,
AND SISTERS AND BROTHERS IN CHRIST.

I LEAVE YOU WITH THIS CHARGE,
FIND OUT WHAT GOD WANTS AND DO THAT.

IN THE WORDS OF HARRY MORGAN,
"I'LL SEE YOU HERE, THERE, OR IN THE AIR!"

Shalom, Shalom,

Big D

CONTACT ME AT
DHAASBIGD@GMAIL.COM

THEOMEGAGENERATION.COM
JUSTHOLDONBOOK.COM